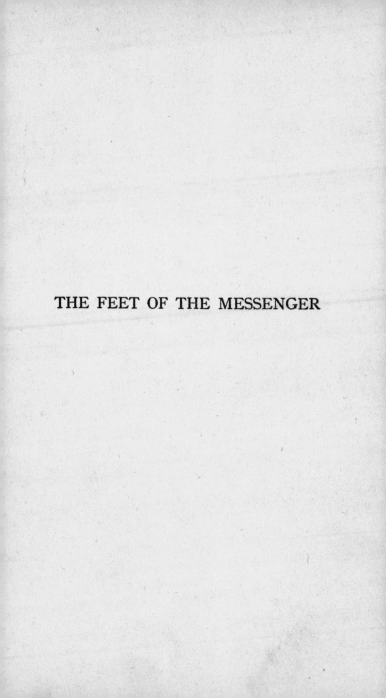

THE FEET OF THE MESSENGER

The
Feet of the Messenger

YEHOASH
[SOLOMON BLOOMGARDEN]

TRANSLATED FROM THE YIDDISH BY
ISAAC GOLDBERG

PHILADELPHIA
THE JEWISH PUBLICATION SOCIETY OF AMERICA
1923

How beautiful upon the mountains
Are the feet of the messenger . . .

— *Isaiah 52. 7.*

CONTENTS

THE REDEMPTION

For a number of years a fond, beautiful dream had been weaving in my thoughts. In a hidden crevice of the soul a seed had taken root and was quietly, modestly burgeoning. Amid the confusion and the tumult of a hundred interests, of labors and ambitions, that seed had remained unobserved. Yet often, in reposeful moments a breath would arise, wafting a sweet fragrance into my face, intoxicating, filling the spirit with sorrow and boundless yearning.

The day arrived when the plant burst all its buds and blossomed forth, spreading and unfolding and enlacing into itself all my thoughts and my most hidden desires. And from that day Eretz Yisroel became for me a luminuous island beckoning at the end of a long, dark journey. Everything good, bright, and beautiful was there upon that island, and I must reach it as soon as possible. Should I ever reach it, all doubts would be resolved, all queries answered, all darknesses illuminated. A new life would begin. A new spring, a new youth, with new, firm beliefs.

As soon as I had resolved upon fulfilling the dream of years, I was thrilled with such a festive mood as I had not felt for long, similar to that holiday spirit which as a child I felt on the eve of Pesah, when I accompanied my father to the synagogue, where all the lamps were lighted and every nook and cranny was bright and tidy, and before my childish thoughts would hover the vision of two feast-nights followed by a long, long Passover.

I was impatient, and suffered greatly from that impatience.

I wanted to wake up one fine morning, in some miraculous manner, and find myself in Eretz Yisroel, in the land of sunshine, as I had begun to call it betimes, even before I had set eyes upon it.

The island of light beamed and beckoned from afar, and I began to count the weeks, the days, the hours.

I set about preparing for the voyage. And regardless of the fact that several months must elapse before my departure, I sped preparations with as much haste and impetuousness as if I were leaving the very next day.

The gangplank was raised and between the huge iron Leviathan and the stout beams of the pier the water began to seethe and froth. The vessel emitted a long frightful roar that made the very railings quiver. All at once—a lurch. The dock, with its hundreds of persons, waving their hats and handkerchiefs, began to recede.

In one corner stood my friends in a group, and as the ship veered and they could no longer see me, they dashed for the outermost edge, so that they might catch a last glimpse. I could see them running, and felt as if they were rushing to seize me and carry me off the ship and then realized that it was too late.

"Never in my life shall I behold those persons and that dock again. Never."

My heart began to sink, as if oppressed by a nightmare, and my eyes grew dim.

Somewhere in the city of Sarajevo, in the Province of Bosnia, a young, impulsive patriot was planning my return—while planning the assassination of the Austrian crown prince that was to bring on the world-war and later to bring me back, on the United States warship "Tennessee", from Jaffa to Alexandria.

But in darkness works the hand that pilots the wheels of fate, and for the moment I beheld slowly disappearing the land that had been my home for the past twenty-three years.

Not a trace of the dock was any longer visible.

I went into my cabin.

All at once I realized how strong were the bonds which linked me to my adopted home. I had grown to love her prairies and her mountains, her lakes and her vast spaces, her gigantic pioneer-spirit, her breadth and her freedom. I felt proud that I was one of her citizens—her free citizens—every one of them a king by grace of his own strength and his own will.

Precious home, that had grown so dear to me! I will think often of you, and will be proud of the twenty-three years during which I trod your free soil, and breathed your free air. I will recall you with love, and bless you, and long for you, but never shall my eyes behold you again.

Through a hundred generations a chain has been formed, and it draws me to a far-off, tiny land. A hundred generations call in my veins and I must answer their summons—but never will I forget you.

Perhaps the bracing winds of your prairies have awakened the dead generations in my blood. Perhaps the majestic peaks of your snow-capped mountains have urged and heartened me to answer the call—who knows?

When I returned to the deck, only a grayish strip could be made out on the horizon—the last sight of land, soon to vanish.

The deck was crowded with couples and individuals who were strolling hither and thither, laughing and chatting. Cold silvery glints sparkled from the sun-spattered waves, and the vessel sped on like a huge swimming bird.

A liveried servant appeared at one of the doors, and blew upon a bugle a sort of military signal—dinner-time.

We entered the dining-saloon. The steward had placed upon our table the flowers that friends had brought or sent to our cabin. All the tables were bedecked uniformly. Flowers cannot endure the sea, and everybody eagerly inhales their fragrance while it lasts.

We have now been on the sea for two days. One by one the bouquets disappear from the tables. Many tables are but half set. The gloom of the bugle that summons to meals grows deeper each time. We now live at the mercy of the ocean.

The steward brought me a pleasant surprise—a Marconigram from New York, and later another from Canada. A hearty hand-clasp across the waves.

The weather is unsettled and dreary.

I gaze far out and see the waves rise and fall, I imagine all manner of things. Now I behold the ruins of a great city washed away by a flood. I can make out the shattered houses, the roofs and the crumbling walls, flowing endlessly on. There comes an entire street that has collapsed, and behind it another and yet another.

A white spot. And the spot grows into a locomotive, whose smoke curls behind a long train of coaches.

A high wave: isn't that the Woolworth Tower of New York?

In an instant everything has vanished.

The ocean is reality. The land is a mirage. Everything that is firm and fixed is an illusion. The world and life are a flux and a change. And the sea is the symbol of that flux and change.

The last sea-gulls have disappeared.

But we are not totally severed from the land. Every morning a newspaper is issued on board, and electric messengers of the air gather news for us from every corner of the world on land and sea.

Save my family, B. and his wife, I know nobody on board. And it looks as if this isolation will last for the rest of the voyage. The passengers are for the most part newly-made millionaires or near-millionaires, who are travelling to Italy or Egypt, bent upon pleasure. Their bearing is by no means unpretending—nothing is more comical than an American parvenu trying to be—as Heine says—"aristokraetzig."

Perhaps this exhibition of snobbery is due to the fact that we are upon an English vessel. I cannot help thinking that an American has too strong a sense of humor to be a snob without self-derision.

Many of the passengers are deeply engrossed in their Baedekers, repeating to themselves, for the tenth time, that "filetto al burro" means beefsteak, and that so innocent a thing as veal-cutlet is called "braciola di vitello".

The cafe is attractive and comfortable. Elderly and young "sports" sit there, drinking, smoking, and playing divers games. All try in every way possible to kill time.

There are several passengers whom I recognize as "Sons of the Covenant". By no means do they care to show this, although they know quite well that we are Jews. That secret must have been revealed to them, if not by my nose, at least by my speech, for with B., who does not know English, I speak Yiddish exclusively. At times, when we wish for a strictly private exchange of views, we speak Hebrew.

Our Hebrew brought us the acquaintance of one who had as little in common as we with the other passengers. He was a Methodist missionary, a tall, gaunt fellow with black side-whiskers and large blue spectacles. He had caught a word or two of our conversation, and waxed quite enthusiastic. Evidently he had not forgotten how profusely he had sweated at the examination upon the two verses of the Psalms assigned to him, and he could not cease marvelling at the ease with which we spoke so difficult a language.

When, later, I arrived at Tel-Aviv, I discovered, much to my consternation, that not all people were such appreciative critics as that clergyman. There were such as evinced no great enthusiasm for my speech; some even had the impudence to say that I spoke Hebrew badly.

The missionary told us that he was journeying as far as Alexandria, and would proceed thence to some place in Africa—to preach the Gospel to woolly-headed natives.

He regarded the pleasure-seekers with intense disgust. I could see that he was scorning them with his bespectacled eyes, and every time I noticed him in the café or in one of the other salons—and he was ubiquitous—it seemed to me that at any moment he would jump upon a chair and begin to pour forth fire and brimstone upon the sinners.

I went down to the second cabin to see whether I couldn't find there a *Jewish* Jew, and possibly, even one who, like me, was on his way to Eretz Yisroel. I met, however, but a handful of passengers, a couple of Italian and Syrian families. There was not a Jewish face to be seen in their midst.

Two years later, when I happened to be in Montreal, a young man came to see me (he had been born in Jerusalem and was now settled in Canada), and asked whether I hadn't met on the *Laconia* a certain old man who was travelling second-class. He was greatly astonished when I answered: "No", and told me, that there was an old man travelling on that ship, and the old man was his father.

Years before the man had come to visit his children in Canada. His intention had been to remain but a short period abroad, and then return to the land of his forefathers whither his heart was ever drawn. But the return voyage would be postponed from one month to the next, from year to year, and in the meantime the man from Jerusalem fell ill and his children absolutely refused to permit him to take the voyage in that condition.

Two years previous, at about the time I had decided to leave America, the old man felt that his end was approaching. Whereupon he entreated his children, by the love they bore him, to send him back to Eretz Yisroel. Let them only take him to the ship. He'd manage to reach the Holy Land.

The doctor declared that he might die any moment. The children with tear-filled eyes, begged him to remain in Montreal and not endanger his life. But the dying man refused to be dissuaded.

He kept repeating: "God that kept me alive in Jerusalem when I dwelt there, will, praised be His name, bring me to Eretz Yisroel. Even though it be but a moment before my death, so that I'll not have to be buried in unhallowed ground".

So his sons brought him to the *Laconia*.

The old man's prayer was not answered. He did not reach the end of his journey. Before the vessel arrived at Gibraltar, the poor old man breathed his last, without anybody near to hear his final confession.

The company delivered the corpse into the care of the small Jewish Kehillah of Gibraltar, and there he was given a Jewish burial.

During all the time that I was listenning to the sad tale about the old man from Jerusalem my thoughts were filled with the wonderful story that I had read in a holy book printed in Jerusalem. The legend recounts that once there dwelt in foreign parts a very wealthy man who was frightfully stingy and cruel. He was exceedingly pious toward God, but to man he was the essence of cruelty. All he cared for was to gather in as much money as possible. With this money he would purchase precious stones and pearls which he had sewed into a leather wallet that he carried next to his heart.

His wife and children, because of his penuriousness, one by one departed this life. They actually starved to death, for he never had given them enough to eat. It may be readily imagined, then, that to strangers he never gave so much as a drink of water.

In his later years, after he had lost his family, he decided to go to Eretz Yisroel. So he settled in Jerusalem. He became even more pious than before, would pray and study for days in succession, and every Friday would weep floods of tears at the Wailing Wall. But toward his fellow-men he continued to be the same heartless wretch as ever. His greatest pleasure was to feel the leather wallet next to his heart. People might die before his very eyes, yet he would not give them the smallest coin. He naturally hated his fellow-men and his animosity grew day by day. He begrudged every one his very life.

When he felt that his end was near, he managed with his last strength to cook himself some soup. Into the soup he cast all the precious stones and pearls that he had been carrying about in his wallet. Then spoonful after spoonful he began to sip the broth together with the jewels, so that after his death, even as during his life, no man might enjoy the possession of them.

As soon as he had swallowed the last diamond, he began to sink, and in a few minutes he died.

His neighbors arrived and charitably buried him in the Jewish cemetery, which is situated upon the Mount of Olives, where the saints and the just have been reposing for tens of centuries.

On the same day, in a tiny hamlet far from Eretz Yisroel, died an old Rabbi, a pure, saintly soul who had never failed to fulfil a divine injunction in every minutest detail. All his life long it grieved him that he could not go to Eretz Yisroel. He was too poor, however, to gratify his desire. And when he died, his last word was "Jerusalem".

After the holy man's burial there was a commotion in the heavenly tribunal. Was this the justice of God? Should a holy man lie in unholy soil because of his poverty, while a cruel, ungodly miser reposed upon the Mount of Olives?

Whereupon a messenger was sent down from heaven, and on that very night the old Rabbi was transported to the holy mountain and the miser took his place.

Sunday morning services were held in the chief salon. On one side sat the passengers and on the other were ranged the sailors, with prayers books in their hands. The services were conducted by the captain, a tall, raw-boned man of about fifty, who rarely appeared upon deck and was held in awe by all the officers and employees, and one of his aides.

The captain kept an eye upon the young sailors, to see whether they were praying. If he caught any one of them pretending, he would eye him severely, even as the Keidaner rebbi would eye me in my childhood days, when I would finish the Eighteen Benedictions in a suspiciously short time.

Our stewardess, a nimble English maid with cheeks as red as apples, observes to me that the sailors would be far more content if they were to receive, instead of a prayer-book, a bottle of Scotch apiece.

On the prayer-books, in large letters, is printed "Cunard Steamship Company", even as on all the other objects of the vessel. That is merely force of habit. It is unnecessary to guard against theft. In any case it is certain that the sailors will not purloin *their* devotionaries.

A step away from the salon, where the sacred hymns were being sung, sat some old sinners in the smoking-room over their soda and brandy, telling each other unholy yarns.

And below, someone was dying.

There is on board a room for gymnastics and every variety of sport.

If one is accustomed to go for a ride every day, the Company has seen to it that he shall not, on that account, become homesick. He is seated upon a sort of make-believe horse, an electric button is pressed, and he gallops away to his heart's content without moving from the spot.

For those who are fond of bicycle riding, or rowing, there is similar provision.

B. happens to be afraid of horses, and has never in his life tasted the pleasure of sitting in a saddle. Yet it is easy to see that his heart has always thirsted for such delights. As soon as he saw the "horse", his eyes lighted up. For the first time in his life he found it possible to satisfy his hidden wish.

He became a passionate devotee of "horse-back riding", and judging from the eagerness with which he bestrode the substitute steed, the man in charge of the room deduced that here was a genuine broncho-buster.

Later he became such a sportsman that mere horse-back riding was no longer sufficient. He went in enthusiastically for bicycling. Since the bicycle didn't stir from the spot, it was hard to tell how fast B. rode. But I am certain that he never made less than sixty miles an hour.

Last night there was a concert in the grand salon. There was singing, recitation, declamation of humor-ous pieces, and jokes that reflected little credit upon the intelligence of the passengers. At the poorest en-tertainment given on the East Side of New York one could have heard better and more genuine wit.

After the concert there was a collection for the orphans and widows of drowned sailors.

One of the passengers, a refined, elderly man, ev-idently a Scotchman, reminded the assembly of the danger one always faces when journeying on the sea, and declared that not even the strongest vessel was absolutely secure against the misfortunes of the deep. The only true protector was the All-merciful One, in whose hands we all were placed, and whose omnipotence we could nowhere escape. Therefore we should ever keep in mind the orphans and widows of those who, like us, rode on the deep and found therein a watery grave.

The night was dark and stormy, and about the tiny round windows of the salon stood thousands of drowned souls, head upon head, counting the collection and wailing.

Besides the four hundred passengers of the first class, who constitute, as may well be understood, the "upper crust", and outside of the few families travelling in the second cabin, there are several hundred Italians between decks. They are homeward bound, and their glee grows daily.

There is a lone Arab, from Syria. He, too, is homeward bound, and has already donned his red fez with its black, dangling tassel. He holds aloof from the Italians. In America it had been necessary to mingle with everybody. Now, however, it's no longer necessary.

When the bell rings for meals there is a merry scurrying from every direction. I wonder why we above haven't such an excellent appetite. And I come to the conclusion that it's all on account of the bugle, which fills us with such gloom.

We are nearing our first stopping-place. One more day and we shall be in beautiful Madeira. The harbingers of land begin to appear—white graceful sea-gulls are circling over translucent waves.

Together with the hot coffee, cold lemonade was served to the passengers—a first token of summer.

One's heart grows joyous and buoyant. Great hopes burgeon forth.

THE LAST LAP

Twenty days after passing the Statue of Liberty, the *Laconia* steamed into the outer harbor of Alexandria. On the afternoon of the same day we re-embarked on the Austrian steamship *Electra*. If I call it steamship it is by way of euphemism. Were I to be realistic, I should call it a tub. I must confess that every time I read that an Austrian ship has been sunk, I console myself with the hope that it is the *Electra*.

Years ago I read the description of a voyage by a renowned Hebrew author, in which he tells of the beautiful thoughts inspired in him as he journeyed upon the *Electra* from Alexandria to Jaffa. The thoughts are really beautiful. But as I boarded the vessel, I found it utterly impossible to understand how such inspirations could occur to a man while travelling on the *Electra*. It seemed to me that the one thought that could come to anybody on that tub was: how to keep from falling over the decrepit railings into the sea.

The ship was ancient and wobbly. The deck was narrow, hardly enough room to move about. The cabins were small, cramped, foul, as if built for the express purpose of testing the endurance of those who were journeying to Eretz Yisroel.

The following morning we reached the key to the Suez Canal, Port Said, where we remained for the whole day. Toward evening the *Electra* weighed its rusty anchor, and left for Jaffa. Sleep was out of the question. I knew that I shouldn't close an eye, and made up my mind to remain on deck as late as possible. Gradually all the other passengers descended to their cabins, and I was left alone.

At the very rim of the horizon, from between two dark clouds, peered a yellow moon like a spectre from the other world. For a moment she vanished, and when she re-appeared she was clear white and cast a weird radiance upon the water.

How many had gone over the same path before me?

The chill midnight air drove me to our cabin, so I lay down and gazed through the port-hole. The first gray glimmer will be the beginning of my first day in Eretz Yisroel, the dawn of a new life. I could hear the waves lapping against the sides of the ship and the boards of the paddle-wheel splashing in the water.

The night dragged slowly on, and no sooner had a patch of pallor tinged the sky than I hastened on deck. The first signs beckoned from afar. Then the shores of Jaffa grew clearer and clearer to the sight, and with the rising of the sun we could make out the yellowish-gray, flat-roofed buildings, which seemed to be heaped one upon the other.

And yonder rose the white houses of Tel-Aviv, as though fresh from their morning bath.

The vessel stopped. We were surrounded by a swarm of rowboats, and the cries of the Arabs in them were deafening. These were the "baharieh", who were to transfer the passengers from the *Electra* to the shore.

When they were not shouting to the passengers, they were yelling at each other, and there arose a din and a pandemonium as if at a shipwreck. Much of the vociferating was not at all necessary, but yelling is second nature to an Arab. The same Arab who is so chary of his words and can sit for hours at a time with sealed lips, rejoices at an opportunity to air his lungs.

"Ya Mahmud! Ya Sa'id! Ya 'Ali!" This at the top of their voices, though Mahmud, Sa'id, and 'Ali were at their very elbow, and would have heard even a whisper.

Before long we and our luggage were rolling in a boat over the restless waters to the "gumruk" (the custom-house).

The shores of Jaffa are ringed with reefs, and ships must anchor far out at sea. It requires great skill on the part of the Arabs to prevent the boats in which they transfer the passengers from colliding with the rocks. During a storm it is impossible to reach shore, and it often happens that because of the inclement weather a ship has to proceed with all passengers to the next port. It also happened that vessels left for the next port, returned, found themselves again unable to land their passengers, went once more on to the next port, came back another time, and were thus shuttlecocked until at last they succeeded in disembarking their passengers.

I sat together with many other passengers listening to the rhythmic song of the "baharieh" as they plied their oars back and forth through the waters. Everything seemed to be floating in a haze.

And now my foot left the rowboat, and stepped upon the earth—upon the earth of Eretz Yisroel.

After my passport had been vised, we were asked two francs per person—a "voluntary" contribution to the Turkish fleet.

My little daughter was too busy with the large doll which she was carrying in her arms to feel any interest in the Turkish fleet, but the customs official decided that she was eager to contribute, and requested her donation of me. Judging from the way the official eyed the doll I could see that he was considering whether or not to inscribe her, too, on the list of donors.

Later, when I had settled down in Rehoboth, I was present when the one-hundred-and-three-year-old Abdallah came to borrow five *bishlik* from Khawaja Musa, for, as he said, the soldiers had come to the village to collect the "voluntary contributions" for the fleet, and beat black and blue anybody who did not give his share.

TEL-AVIV

During the entire time we drove from the "Gumruk" through the streets of Jaffa a thin drizzle had been falling. As we entered Tel-Aviv the rain ceased. The sky had cleared entirely, and golden sunlight was everywhere reflected from the white walls and the window-panes, and pouring down upon the well-swept sidewalks and paved streets.

I had been told that Tel-Aviv was the banner-town of the New Settlement. It seemed that the statement contained more truth than fiction.

In every direction the eye was greeted with the two bright colors of the Zionist flag: white and blue. Below, white, dazzling white houses; above, blue, dazzling blue heavens, and in the background, a blue, deep blue sea.

No half-tints, no nuances, neither timidity nor indecision—nothing but clear, bright hues that burst upon one like trumpet blasts.

All at once my head and my heart grew as clear and serene as the skies overhead. The flood of sunlight and the festive tidiness all about were greetings to me. I knew this as surely as I knew that I had come to Eretz Yisroel.

Everything spoke to me, sang to me.

We passed by an old barefoot Arab who was leading a loaded camel. *His* forefathers for I don't know how many generations back had surely driven camels and grazed their sheep on this selfsame spot, and had pitched here their black tents, lighting fires at evening, baking "pittes", and afterward sitting around the fire telling stories in the tranquil night.

I—had only just arrived, from a distant land—had not yet slept a night in Eretz Yisroel—had not yet drunk a glass of water in it, not yet walked ten paces upon its soil, and yet—

I felt more rooted here than he. *I* was the long established dweller. From the blood there leaped the muffled clamor of centuries: "My Birthright".

We entered Rehob Herzl and reached Rothschild Square, where an arch of triumph had been erected, festooned with palm-branches and flowers. This was in preparation for the visit of Baron Edmond de Rothschild, who was to arrive that morning.

We stopped at an hotel at the corner of Rehob Herzl and Rehob Ahad ha-'Am, exactly opposite the High School—a tall, simple white edifice with two miniature towers in the middle. The High School is the centre and the pride of Tel-Aviv. As one enters the village the first welcome is extended by this institution, as if it were to say: "Know ye that all the houses ye see and all the persons on the streets were created for me alone. I am all-important here."

The whole village is astir with preparations for the Baron's reception. The leading representatives of the High School and the chief citizens are in a fever of excitement. Every moment messengers arrive with new tidings: the Baron's yacht may be descried from afar, the yacht has already anchored, and so on.

In honor of the Baron's coming the High School students have been granted a holiday. The streets are thronged with them. Handsome, sturdy youths and maidens. Their language is Hebrew. They laugh and chat, jest and chase one another about.

Here comes a pretty Jewish maiden speeding by on a bicycle, disappearing around a corner.

Carriages dash hither and thither and the bells upon the horses tinkle unceasingly. The coach that takes you from Tel-Aviv to Jaffa for two *metallik* cannot accommodate all the passengers.

Flags are flying from the houses, and the crowd grows momentarily denser.

To-day is Friday. The Baron has not arrived, and will not come until Sunday. In the meantime the Sabbath-eve dusk descends upon the village. The coach is no longer running, the carriages have disappeared. There is no trace now of the week-day atmosphere.

The sun has already set. Soft shadows spread more and more thickly, the heavens are strewn with stars, and the streets teem with young couples and groups, who saunter along in every direction. Through the open windows streams of light pour forth from the houses, and here and there a song bursts forth with the light. The words and the melodies are so familiar, so intimate.

Men and women sit upon the verandas in the semi-darkness, breathing the cool evening air, chatting, and upon everything and everybody is shed the chaste spirit of the Sabbath.

They tell me that not long ago it was the custom to lower the gate in Tel-Aviv on the Sabbath, and no vehicle or horse was allowed to desecrate the holy day of rest. Now it is not permitted to lower the barrier. But rarely does a carriage or a rider drive through on the Sabbath.

As to Jews, that is a foregone conclusion. Even the most reckless violator of "Yom-Kippur" would think twice before he would venture publicly to desecrate the Sabbath.

There was a certain woman who tried to work in her garden on Sabbath, and she was almost lynched. And not at all—God forbid!—by Jews with long ear-locks but by—young students from the Hebrew High School.

These same youths on another occasion besieged the house where a noted Jewish author was staying, and would not allow him to go to a lecture that he was supposed to deliver in Yiddish. Another time they did something that required less heroism. For that very reason, however, it was of quicker and more decisive effect.

They launched a "chemical obstruction" in a theatre where the Yiddishists—who have as much chance in Tel-Aviv as the Hebraists in Chicago—were producing a play in Yiddish.

For the benefit of those who do not know what a "chemical obstruction" is, I will simply note that it is

a method of argumentation more convincing to the
olifactory organ than to reason, and consists in the
use of such ingredients as even the martyred nose of a
Yiddishist cannot endure.

At last the Baron arrived. A multitude of some four
or five thousand persons assembled. Order was preserved by the members of the Maccabean Athletic
Club. Linking hands, they formed a chain behind the
Baron's carriage and bravely stemmed the thousand-
headed throng that pressed with all its might to break
through.

The news of the Baron's coming had spread also to
the Arabian quarter of Jaffa.

With that gift of nicknaming possessed by all Arabs,
they called the Baron "Abu'l-Masari", the father of
money. Others called him, more poetically, "Abu'l-
Sunduk", the father of the coffer.

I saw the "Abu'l-Sunduk" standing upon a balcony,
gazing down upon the vast crowd that had come to
render him homage. He was deeply moved. His old
face beamed with genuine joy.

Fifteen years before, when he had come to Palestine,
he had met colonists who looked to him for aid and a
community that depended upon his benefactions,
which were distributed by dishonest or incapable
administrators. Now he found independent pioneers
who greeted him with sincere love and admiration, but
without mendicant humility. They expected nothing
of him. They had come together to rejoice with him
at the splendid fruit that had sprung from the seed

which he and others had sown with such great effort
and with such heavy heart.

He was especially delighted with those settlements
and colonies in the upbuilding of which he himself had
played no part. He, whose sole dream for three suc-
cessive decades had been the colonization of Jews in
Palestine, knew better than any other how to appreciate those results which had been accomplished
without his aid.

Tel-Aviv was altogether a revelation to him. But
here and there a dark thread was visible. In Rishon
l'Zion, they say, the Baron asked: "How does it happen that I meet in Paris so many sons of Eretz Yisroel
colonists?"

In Ekron—perhaps the most backward of the colonies in Judea—the Baron was welcomed by a chorus
of children singing Hebrew songs. He noticed that
some of the little ones had sore eyes, and asked whether
instead of teaching the children singing, it wouldn't be
far better to give their eyes a good wash.

When the Baroness was invited to the Music School
of Tel-Aviv, she remarked: "Vous commencez tou-
jours par le dessert." (You always begin with the
dessert.)

Despite all the elaborate arrangements made in his
honor, the "Abu'l-Sunduk" remained in Tel-Aviv a
couple of hours only. He was in a hurry to leave for
Jerusalem.

HERZLIAH

Yesterday evening I attended a *neshef* (*soirée*) at the Herzliah High School. Baron de Rothschild, who had been expected, did not appear, but it was foreordained that the evening should not pass without the presence of an "Abu'l-Sunduk". There arrived the Chicago multi-millionaire and philanthropist, Mr. R. and his wife.

The spacious hall of the High School was filled to overflowing with boy and girl students and invited guests. The program consisted of choral singing, recitations, an orchestra of wind instruments, a mandolin orchestra, and, finally, gymnastics. The performers were students.

The pupils that took part in the closing number went through all of their figures with vigor, skill, and rare grace. They were all lithe, broad-chested youths, dressed in white trousers and striped sweaters of white and blue. On each one's bosom was embroidered the word "Herzliah", the name of the High School.

An excellent poem by Frischmann was read, but in the Sephardic Hebrew pronunciation the lines lost their original rhythm.

The problem of retaining in the Sephardic accent the rhythm of Hebrew songs composed originally in the

Ashkenazic pronunciation will be very hard for the
devotees of the *ha-Havarah ha-Sefardit* to solve. Yet
practically all residents in EretzYisroel use exclusively
this latter. The most sonorous strophes of Bialik and
Shneor must naturally lose the greater part of their
melody when uttered in the Sephardic pronunciation.
No wonder then that many Hebrew authors in foreign
countries look askance at the *ha-Havarah ha-Sefardit*.
One of them — a well-known mystic and philosopher,
who never in his life cracked a joke—perpetrated his
first and only pun at the expense of the selfsame dialect calling it *ha-Havarah ha-Sefarde'it*, the language
of the frogs.

And yet, after residing in Eretz Yisroel for an appreciable length of time, one begins to feel that the Sephardic accent is the proper one, despite all historico-
philological considerations.

The Chicago millionaire was evidently very little
concerned about the matter of accent. He applauded
all recitations indiscriminately out of purely philan-
thropic motives. He was genuinely and heartily
pleased, however, with the gymnastic part of the
program. During the whole time that the young
Jewish athletes went through their various physical
exercises to the accompaniment of a small harmo-
nium, he did not remove his eyes from them. He
went into ecstasies over every turn and twist, and
applauded with the enthusiasm of a boy. In addition to his applause he contributed five hundred
dollars toward a tennis-court for the students.

When the same millionaire visited a certain educational institution in Jerusalem—I was told—the people were no longer content with ovations, and they carried him on their shoulders. For the honor of my millionaire compatriot I should like to believe that he put up a vigorous resistance and that he kicked out a few teeth of some of those enthusiasts.

And it occurs to me that wonderful bargains may be found in Eretz Yisroel. If the Lord blesses anyone with heaps of money and he is eager to purchase honor, let him at once take a trip to Palestine. What must cost a fortune in New York, Chicago, or Boston may be bought for a song in the land of our forefathers.

It was quite late when the program came to an end and the audience dispersed.

For a long time afterward I sat leaning against my window, and the High School students marched through the quiet streets of Tel-Aviv, lustily singing Hebrew songs into the starry night.

"MISTRESS AND MAID"*

Yiddish here is taboo. To speak Yiddish in public requires the utmost courage.

Students from the seventh and the eighth classes often come over to visit me. I try to converse with them in Hebrew. God in heaven knows that my intentions are of the best, but my tongue is still awkward. So I begin to speak Yiddish. Whereupon they, too, speak Yiddish. Some of their companions or perhaps an instructor in the High School or an ordinary pedestrian happen to pass by; they make a wry face at me and my friends. Have I come here to spread apostasy?

The old veteran of the settlement, hoary-headed Eisenstadt, meets me and inquires whether it is true that I have come for the purpose of publishing a "Jargon" newspaper in Palestine. I assure him that such a horrible crime could never have occurred to me even in a dream. He makes a grimace betokening that he believes me in all good faith, smiles, and says that never in his life would he have harbored such a suspicion against me. He has merely repeated to me what others said. Yet I see that his mind was not quite at rest on that score.

One can never feel too secure with these fellows that write "Jargon."

A merchant, to whom Mr. G. introduces me as a "Jargon writer", asks me with genuine pity whether I am not ashamed to write "Jargon". I take my life

*These two terms are employed by the Maskilim to denote Hebrew and Yiddish, respectively.

in my hands and answer: "No". I notice that his face darkens, and his former pity sours to scorn. And he had thought all the while that I was penitent!

A young girl, evidently a recent arrival in Tel-Aviv, stops me in the thoroughfare, and asks me in a mutilated Hebrew to direct her to a certain place. I don't answer quickly enough, from which she infers that I do not understand her Hebrew. She is embarrassed and asks again—in a sorry Russian.

"But why don't you ask in your mother-tongue?" I exclaim in good Lithuanian Yiddish. It was as if I had brought new life to the maiden, and she began to speak in a Yiddish which I hope the Lord would confer upon a great many of our younger Yiddish writers.

Yiddish in Tel-Aviv! Is such a thing possible?—So the poor thing had to worry along in Russian.

I watched a group of young students playing football. There were the usual cries and wrangles, but not even during the most heated moments of the game did a non-Hebrew word escape their lips. To me this was the best proof that the language had entered their very soul! and had grown to be an organic part of them. A great victory for the pioneers of the linguistic renaissance.

On the other hand, the older people, though they speak Hebrew fluently, reveal a great deal of artificiality, a great deal of constraint, as if they would say: "We have resolved upon a thing, and we will carry it through, no matter how difficult it may be". Most of the conversations, or at least, those that I happened to hear, are generally flat, and restricted to a single, trite circle of ideas. Few jokes are told, and lively humor is altogether lacking. This I ascribe to the unnaturalness of their Hebrew speech. It seems as if the moment they would begin to speak Yiddish, they would commence to breathe more freely, and to speak more interestingly, with greater zest and more humor.

Then there are the very aged Jews who make such piteous endeavors to speak Hebrew. If it weren't that they were ashamed, they would talk Yiddish, but somehow or other that would look bad before the young folks. So they break their teeth in the attempt, lest they should be laughed at, precisely as the older Jewish folks in America labor with their broken English.

But this is Eretz Yisroel, and the ardent effort is made willingly. The parents look at their own children, and hear how sweetly and naturally *they* speak Hebrew, and their hearts melt with joy.

As to the language itself, it is not an insurmountable difficulty. But that Sephardic accent! A pious old Jew told me with a sigh that he had tried, in every manner possible, to recite his prayers in *ha-Havarah ha-Sefardit*, but that his tongue stuck to the roof of his mouth and he simply could not utter the words. Wherefore he had resolved that as far as intercourse with men on the streets was concerned—well and good; but as to the synagogue, good old Shnipishok Hebrew for him.

One day I arose at early dawn. There was hardly a soul to be seen on the street. The donkey laden with fresh rolls from Katz's *Ma'afiyyah* (bakery) had only just gone by, which was a sign that it was still very early.

I noticed an elderly Jew with a grayish beard thrust his head through a window, look about him in every direction, and greet someone whom he had evidently just seen with a hearty "Gut Morgen". As he did so, the man smacked his lips with delight. Joy was written all over his face. He had slipped in a Yiddish word.

Even more to be pitied were the "enforced converts" who, because of stern business necessity have had to adopt the faith of Tel-Aviv. Of such was the young man in the *Masperah* (barber-shop) where I went to get my hair cut. At first he expended upon me the few Hebrew words and phrases that he had so evidently committed to memory by dint of hard labor. When, however, he discovered that I would not betray him, he divulged his identity in fluent Yiddish.

The only outspoken Yiddishists that have the courage of their convictions are the Arabs who visit Tel-Aviv to sell their wares. Here comes a tall, thin Arab, leading a tiny donkey laden with earthen vessels, crying beneath the very windows of the High School in classic Yiddish: "Tel–er–lekh, te–pe–lekh, shis–e–lekh!" (saucers, pots, and dishes). And from the other end of the street comes an Arab woman with a basket of oranges on her head, singing in a half-melancholy, half-angry strain, "Gute maranzi, maranzi gute! Maranzi!"

And yet, however ridiculous and petty the hostility of local enemies to Yiddish is, it is quite natural. For years and years these people have labored, fought and struggled with all their might, making every sort of sacrifice to revive the ancient tongue; they have thought by day and dreamed by night of this revival. And now, when they behold the first fruit of their labor, how can one expect them to be tolerant toward the language that they consider the most dangerous rival of their ideal?

Personally I find myself daily believing more and more in the possibility of reviving the language of our forebears in Eretz Yisroel. Hebrew has always been a necessity in Palestine as a universal tongue in which Jews that come hither from every corner of the earth have been able to understand one another. The Jew from Persia and the Jew from Afghanistan, the Jew from Germany and the Jew from Yemen, were obliged to use Hebrew in order to find a brother in one another. This necessity becomes daily stronger, and will provide a constant incentive to the employment of Hebrew. In time Hebrew can become as natural to the residents of Palestine as it was to our ancestors two thousand years ago.

After all, Hebrew has always been an important element in all the dialects that Jews have adopted in the various lands where they were dispersed. Perhaps in a sense one might even call Yiddish a Hebraic dialect.

On the other hand, I often think what an immense store of valuable pioneer energy is expended upon the *language* in Eretz Yisroel. And I recall what Heine once said: "If the Romans had first been obliged to learn Latin, they would have had no time to conquer the world."

At our boarding-house there are several students from the higher classes in the High School. They come from Russia, they studied in the high schools of that country, and came to Tel-Aviv to continue their education.

Every morning I hear them repeating their lessons. One of them is studying his Latin lesson in Hebrew— dead Latin in living Hebrew.

My heart swells with pride, and I say to myself: "Jerusalem has conquered Rome."

What language the sea speaks in Tel-Aviv I don't know, but I could never tire of listening to it. The day is all too short. In the morning I stand on the golden sands and watch the blue waves of the Mediterranean lash and break upon the craggy shore and the snow-white foam glisten in the sunlight.

I am often accompanied by the Hebrew poet F., and we both contemplate the sea and the sky with ecstasy; our joy knows no bounds. Our conversations are a part of the surrounding gladness.

He says to me: "Do you know, I don't feel like writing a line here. Why create beautiful things, when the world about you is so beautiful and radiant?"

He has taken the words out of my mouth.

I feel at home with the sea, and forget the disgrace of being a "Jargon writer" and spreading apostasy (God forbid!) among innocent Jewish youth. I am happy, supremely happy, to be in Eretz Yisroel.

At night the heavens are studded with stars, and out of the darkness comes the sound of the roaring, thundering sea. I know that it is roaring and thundering at the birth of a nation, of a great dream in process of realization.

Suddenly I am seized with a sweet pain and a languor, and old wounds begin to bleed.

SUNSHINE

The keynote of Tel-Aviv is sunshine, a flood of sunshine, which inundates the roofs, pours down from the roofs over the walls, splashes from the walls to the young trees, whose tender roots delve into the sandy soil for a little moisture, scatters over the street and the yellow heaps of sand, and is shattered into golden spangles upon the sapphire-blue expanse of the sea.

Sunshine, a flood of sunshine, is likewise the fundamental note of life itself in Tel-Aviv.

Among the instructors of the High School, among the students, in the boarding-house, in the Anglo-Palestine Bank—everywhere the air is permeated with radiant hopes, with plans for the future, with the spirit of enterprise, with self-confidence and faith in success.

The Palestinian Bureau, which is situated on the upper story of our boarding-house, is besieged from early morning till late at night by monied persons who have come to purchase land. Capital, which is by nature wary, and usually sends ahead of it its servant —labor—to spy out new territory, has begun to appear in *propria persona*, not merely to take a look and run off, but really to stay. The settlement has commenced to be looked upon as a good business investment.

The city merchant who is not enough of a pioneer to become a colonist, and not idealist enough to sac-

rifice his city comforts to his love for Eretz Yisroel—
this city merchant may now dwell in a modern structure, enjoy all comforts, even more than his city life has
accustomed him to, may send his sons and daughters
to High School, find a profitable investment for his
capital and his energy, and at the same time dwell in
the land of his fathers.

The toilers who have come hither to "eat bread with
salt, and drink water by measure"—to offer up every
sort of sacrifice for the nation and land—naturally
regard these bourgeois with hostility. Nor are there
lacking piquant tales about certain settlers who have
come to Eretz Yisroel to purify their ill-gotten gains.
Rumors are current of business ventures, of new
American colonies, of every sort of enterprise. There
are tales of new land purchases, both by individuals
and groups.

In a single day I heard of five purchases, each in-
volving thirty thousand *dunam*. But it was not given
to me to enjoy these glad tidings for long. It transpired
that in each case the same thirty thousand *dunam*
were referred to, only by different mouths, and finally
nothing came of the matter. As it turned out, there
had only been negotiations with the Arab land-owners.

Two Chicago Jews have arrived with a plan to open
a clothing factory in Jerusalem. According to their
figures the business will be a highly profitable one.
They count in particular upon low wages. Besides
this, the apprentices to the trade will at first receive
no pay, so that their labor will be all profit. These two

Jews have already leased a house near the Bezalel Institute, and intend very shortly to clothe Jerusalem with their products.

What a happy day for the Palestinian settlement when the whir of Singer machines will announce to the residents of Jerusalem that the "sweat-shop" has arrived.

At every turn there are signs of good times. There are even stories of professional beggars who have journeyed all the way from Odessa to pursue their vocation in Tel-Aviv.

In the Anglo-Palestine Bank, which is situated not in Tel-Aviv, but right in the centre of the filthy Arab quarter of Jaffa, there is din as at an annual fair. At every window there is a pushing crowd. Persons have come to deposit money, to buy and exchange money orders, loan money, to redeem notes, and so on.

The official language of the bank is Hebrew. A placard asks the public to speak Hebrew. Those who can, do so. The bank stationery is in Hebrew. The inscriptions over the clerks' windows are in Hebrew. The customers are all Jews with the exception of a few important Arab merchants who do business through the bank with Jews, or keep their money there for safety.

The bank, established by Jews *for* Jews, pays particular attention to Jewish needs and Jewish methods of businees and finance, and the Jewish merchant feels more at home there than he could feel in even the most friendly non-Jewish bank under the most favorable conditions. From one direction flows a constant stream of new funds into the bank. The bank pays five per cent on yearly deposits, and the guarantee of the entire Jewish nation—which every depositor more or less believes to see behind the bank—attracts Jewish money from every corner. From the other direction comes a constant demand for funds to finance new enterprises, land-purchases, to pay for machinery, and so on. A great deal of money pours forth in a golden stream from the Anglo-Palestine Bank to fructify all the industries of the new settlement.

I take up a position near the *Kuppah*, or cashier's window. I have an order to exchange. The line is long and the cashier is none too quick. Just as my turn has come, a fellow appears from the opposite direction and approaches the window.

I ask the cashier:

"How is this? I've been waiting in line for over fifteen minutes."

I am on the point of getting angry, when an elderly Jew, with a long, genuine Isaiah beard, and with mild, Jewish eyes—evidently a business man of the old type —turns toward me, and takes me by the sleeve:

"Young man, why so vexed? After all, we're in Eretz Yisroel, and we're all Jews, praise be to God. Sooner, later—what's the difference? You'll get there all right."

If I had heard such an argument in the Chemical National Bank of New York, I would have done

one of two things; either I would have thrust the old man aside, or I should have burst into laughter.

But here I really saw that the old fellow was right. I had not sailed across the ocean to stand upon my right of "next".

I enter a private office, and see, before a long desk littered with documents, Mr. G. the compiler of Hebrew text-books and dictionaries, and at the same time one of the officials of the Anglo-Palestine Bank.

He offers me a chair beside him, and asks one of the bank employees to fetch coffee.

In the meantime in comes one man and out goes the other. The lexicographer does not rest for a moment; he counter-signs checks, signs documents, makes loans, asks questions and answers them—and in between he manages to discuss the new dictionary on which he has been working a long time.

Before my eyes, promptly and accurately, business is transacted that involves many tens of thousands of francs. A man enters with a bill of lading and wishes the bank to pay for the goods that have come to him and hold it in the bank's warehouse. A colonist from Pethach Tikvah needs money with which to purchase crates for his oranges, and the head of a small colony has come to borrow money from the bank for the purpose of installing a water system.

The author of Hebrew text-books knows such customers intimately—the history, family connections, condition and prospects, capabilities and habits of every applicant. On the strength of this knowledge he decides whom to favor and whom to refuse, and indicates the individual extent of credit. He is the bank's "Bradstreet".

He takes advantage of a free moment, and extracts from a desk-drawer the proof-sheets of the "Alef" section of his dictionary.

I look over the proof-sheets, sip slowly my thimbleful of coffee, and the Evil One once more brings to my mind thoughts of the Chemical National Bank of New York.

But I scoff at the tempter. In Eretz Yisroel the taunts of the Evil One have no effect.

At the other end of the spacious office, likewise before a desk littered with documents, sits another official of the bank—a tall, thin, brown-skinned Sephardi, wearing a red fez with a black tassel.

His duty is to receive the Arab merchants and *effendis* who do business with the bank. An Arab enters in a black, flowing gown, with a white turban on his head, and greetings are exchanged.

The Sephardi rises, and each party, with the utmost ceremoniousness, places his right hand first over his heart and then upon his forehead. Then one of them says:

"Naharak sa'id" (May your day be happy).

Whereupon the other replies:

"Naharak sa'id umubarak" (May your day be happy and blessed).

Then the turbaned Sephardi offers his guest cigarettes and orders coffee. They sit down around the huge desk, smoke and take small sips of the viscous bever-

age, and between puffs and sips go over the same rout-
ine ground of question and answer:

"Kif halak" (How are you?).

"El-Hamdu lillah" (thanks to Allah).

They converse upon every conceivable topic, and
incidentally they transact the business which is the
purpose of the meeting.

In imposing privacy sits the chief director of the
bank—a tall, broad-shouldered Jew in spectacles,
with a long, grayish-brown beard. His first appearance upon the stage of Palestinian Colonization was
made about twenty-five or thirty years ago—as the
author of a Hebrew book on Eretz Yisroel. Now he
is the head representative of a bank that has assets
of about nine million francs. If he had worn a skull-
cap, I could easily have taken him for a Shohet from
an East-European town. But his exposed bald head
destroyed this illusion. Instead of addressing me in
Hebrew or in Yiddish, he *tried* to speak to me in
English. The attempt was very unsuccessful, and I
at once recognized the Maskil.

By this time it is half-past twelve. The bank is
emptied. The employees leave their little windows
and hurry out of the place. The doors are closed. They
will not re-open for two hours.

Together with Mr. G. I return to Tel-Aviv.

As we approach my boarding-house the lexico-
grapher-pedagogue-bank official bids me a hurried
good-bye: "I want to get in a half-hour's work on the
dictionary."

AROUND THE TABLE

The tourist season is not yet in full swing—it won't be till Passover. But at our boarding-house the tables are almost always occupied. Shloyme, the barefoot Yemenite (he wears shoes only in honor of the Sabbath, weighs seventy-five pounds in all, including his high red fez, and does enough work for three), finds it impossible to serve all the guests, so that the proprietress, the widow of a Rehoboth pioneer, and her children must come to his assistance.

Near me sits the sewing instructress of the *Bet Sefer le-Banot* (Girls' School), a tall middle-aged spinster. I can't imagine what I could have said to bring such frightful thoughts into her mind; but she has taken it into her head that I poke fun at her. I may converse with her upon the most serious and most innocent matters, and show myself as frank and friendly as one may be toward an elderly spinster; yet she has lost all faith in me.

When I tell her what tall buildings there are in New York, she makes a wry face and says: "I understand what you're driving at". And she turns away from me with an indignant expression. She appears to be a worthy Jewish daughter, and I am sincerely distressed that she should have taken a dislike to me.

Opposite us sits the young physician—a thin chap with a tiny blond mustache and dull eyes that gaze gloomily down into his plate. Next to him sits his wife, a diminutive brunette with sweet, velvety eyes. During the meal they do not speak to us, nor to each other. As soon as they have eaten their prunes—our dinner always concludes with prunes—they rise from the table and disappear into their room which at the same time is the office where the doctor receives, or is supposed to receive, patients,

This physician arrived not very long ago from somewhere in Poland. He is a *Rofe le-mahalat ha-'azabbim*, (neurologist), but from his melancholy manner one may guess that the denizens of Tel-Aviv possess iron nerves. In the meantime the couple live upon the dowry which the physician received in addition to the velvety eyes.

Not far from our table sits a young couple from Lithuania. Both eat lots of bread, and are embarrassed when Shloyme asks them what kind of *marak* they'll have. They don't know a word of the Holy Tongue, and feel downcast. I should like to console them and say that the Lord's mercy is great and as long as a man's intentions are good it makes no difference even if he speaks Yiddish. But I tremble at the thought of the sewing instructress. Shloyme, however, who exerts every ounce of his Yemenite strength to learn Yiddish, promptly corrects himself and asks them: "What kind of soup?" and the Lithuanian couple acquire a new lease of life.

Near them sits the tall Jew from Petrograd, one of the former publishers of the Russian newspaper "Niva." He is half deaf, and before you can get into conversation with him you must shout into his ears. It is a

long time since he has lived among Jews, and he goes
into ecstasies over everything Jewish, including the
Jewish dishes that Shloyme serves him. Everything
is to him a symbol of the Jewish renaissance—even
the chopped liver and radish that our landlady serves
as an appetizer.

The High School student, the son of a Warsaw
business-man (who has been in the same class for two
years, despite the fact that he is a very industrious
student), looks at us out of red, idiotic eyes. He doesn't speak a word except the daily greeting "Shalom".

On the other hand, the woman who has a drug-store
in Kovno, and has come hither to discover whether
she could move her business to Tel-Aviv, speaks without let-up, and in German at that, with an *Aleksott*
accent. She is either a divorcée or a widow, and is
evidently on the look-out for a match.

At one of the tables sit the star-boarders. At their
head is Dr. Z., a bachelor well along in years, who has
come from Switzerland, where he took his degree as
doctor of philosophy. He is the instructor in Talmud
and other subjects at the Herzliah. He is utterly
engrossed in his work. A modern reincarnation of the
old-time teacher. I like him for his earnestness and his
upright idealism, and on that account forgive him his
hostility to Yiddish and his limited acquaintance with
matters that lie without the radius of his school and its
activities. Like all the other teachers in the High
School, he looks upon that institution as the keystone
of the settlement. The instructors regard each other,

in more or less naive fashion, as the sole true builders of the Jewish future.

This very look of scorn upon all things not pertaining to the Herzliah, has been caught by the students from their instructors. The most modest pupil looks upon himself as a eminent pillar of the new Jewish life. This exaggerated pride is responsible for a great deal of insolence on the part of the students.

Near Dr. Z. sits the pretty book-keeper. She knows that all eyes are turned upon her plump arms and her large black orbs, but pretends not to be aware of anything.

The two green-faced maidens, instructresses in the *Gan* (kindergarten), and occupying seats near her, are very plainly envious, but conceal their envy with an extra dose of friendliness toward their beautiful table companion.

Then there are two members of the city council of the colony Hederah, who have come on some matter of communal importance. One of them, a very aged-looking Jew of about forty, with half-bare gums and the marks of week-long fevers carved into his cheeks, tells me that I simply must pay a visit to Hederah. There is not a colony in the world as pretty and precious as this one. He is one of the first who settled in the swampy district. One by one, family after family, the greater part of the brave pioneers succumbed to the malignant fever, until an entire cemetery was filled with their graves. Those who survived did not give up the fight.

In the marshy soil they planted eucalyptus-trees, and the thirsty eucalypti sucked in the pestilential moisture; the air became pure and now fever-worn colonists may come to Tel-Aviv and praise their beautiful Hederah.

I stand at the window and gaze out upon the stream of students and ordinary pedestrians that flows by our boarding-house.

Is a Jewish melting-pot slowly forming here? Not in externals, at least.

I am shocked by the diversity of the garments. It is as though everybody had purposely resolved to retain his native garb from Russia, Galicia, Germany, and other countries.

This diversity offends one's eye, particularly in the students of the High School. If they do not wear uniforms, their clothes ought at least to be restricted within the bounds of a certain grade of uniformity.

I was scandalized by two pupils, who were dressed in uniforms of Russian *gymnasia*.

Moreover, as in a great many other particulars, so in the matter of clothing, everybody in Eretz Yisroel airs all those hidden romantic notions that he would in other places either be ashamed or afraid to display openly.

Recently I met the young writer S. He was wearing a pair of stiff, shining, red riding-boots. I asked him whether he rode a horse. He answered "No, but it feels better to walk in these riding-boots."

I explain the matter to myself in the following way: This chap probably dreamed in his childhood of owning a pair of riding-boots such as he had seen the gentry of his town wear; that dream of the riding-boots slumbered for years and decades, until he came to Tel-Aviv and resolved to realize his leathern dream.

For the same reason, perhaps, a certain professor of an art school in Jerusalem carries a riding-whip with him wherever he goes.

In the colony, on the other hand, there is a tendency to get rid gradually of the European garments and change them for Arabian clothes. The working people and particularly the *Shomerim* (riding watchman), are very fond of dressing like Bedouins. After all, Bedouin dress is not only very graceful, but very comfortable as well. The drooping head-covering is a necessary protection against the sun's scorching rays, and the loose cloak is pleasant to wear, and allows one's limbs free and easy movement.

Those who do not possess a complete Bedouin outfit procure a table cloth or a towel somewhere, gird it about with a black curtain cord and "play Bedouin".

BUILDING

The former associate publisher of the *Niva* asked me to accompany him on a visit to the High School. Dr. M. received us very cordially, and asked which class we should like to visit.

Since I know that the Petrograd fellow, begging his pardon, was quite ignorant of things Jewish, and that in addition to this, he was half deaf, and that it was not the custom to shout lessons in the Herzliah through a megaphone, I was at first somewhat embarrassed. I desired that this man who is returning to the fold should carry away the best possible impression of the institution. But how can this be accomplished, if the man is deaf?

I had an inspiration. I shall take him to the gymnastic class. So I told Dr. M. that *we* should like to see the class in gymnastics. If he cannot hear, let him at least see. Well, as ill-luck would have it, there wasn't any class in gymnastics that day. There was nothing left but to take the deaf Petrogradian to any class at all.

I selected the Bible class, where Dr. M. was lecturing on the forty-fifth Psalm: "My heart overfloweth with goodly matter." We were placed amongst the students, copies of the Psalms were given us, and the lesson began.

The hour taken up by the lesson fled by for me like a minute. I forgot my companion and the whole High School. Under the spell of the beautiful interpretation given by the lecturer the verses began to quiver with colorful animation.

The students hung upon the instructor's lips; this attention was not forced or perfunctory, but the result of sincere and keen enjoyment.

On another occasion Dr. Z. invited me to attend his Talmud class. The text was the Mishnah, the section "Possession of houses", in Baba Batra: "Mere possession does not necessarily constitute property right".

Dr. Z. explained in fluent Hebrew to his students the juridical principle of *Hazakah*, and why *Hazakah*, or the mere fact that one happened to be in possession of a certain thing, was not in and by itself enough to establish one's right to it as property. Such possession must be also fortified by a certain logical justification.

My memory leaped backward a couple of decades and transported me to a cramped, low, little room. The tiny room lacked a floor and in the middle stood a long, wooden table. At the end, upon a worn out chair sat an old, bent Jew with a white beard, swaying back and forth over an ancient Gemara. On either side, on long benches, sat about ten youngsters swaying back and forth together with their teacher, repeating what he was chanting. A small portion they understood, and the greater part they did not even begin to understand, and all the time the little school-room resounded with: "Mere possession does not necessarily constitute property right."

In one of these youngsters I recognized the man now listening to Dr. Z. with head uncovered and clean shaven face, expounding the juridical principles of possession to a silent, attentive class.

My imagination might perhaps have been able to transform the youths and even the girls into the youngsters of a couple of decades back—the small desks into a long, unpainted table, the well-scoured mosaic-plaster into the floor of dirty earth, the bare head of Dr. Z. into my old teacher's feather-covered skull-cap. But I was prevented by the Sephardic accent. The "pathah" against which I have a prejudice of old was so often repeated in the words *Hazakah* and *Tanna*, and so on, that my imagination could in no way transform the Talmud-instructor of the Herzliah into the Gemara-teacher of my childhood who pronounced these vowels like *o*.

In answering the question put to his students by Dr. Z.; a sixteen-year old girl, with black, deeply earnest eyes, rose brilliantly above the others of the class.

Instruction is given to both sexes together. Young boys and girls sit close to each other on the same bench. The founders and the teachers of the institution have evidently imbibed all their notions of education from Switzerland, where the majority of them took their doctor's degrees, and believe that one must always begin with the "last word".

In the United States, where relations between the sexes in ordinary life is freer, I believe, than in any other country in the world, the co-educational system is still in its experimental stages, and perhaps it would not have been amiss if the Tel-Aviv school were not in such a hurry to introduce a system that may be interpreted as rather the ultra-radicalism of the former Yeshiva bohur than as a sign of healthy progressiveness.

I visited the Labor Bureau that the Poale-Zionists maintain in Jaffa.

The influx of colonists has increased considerably of late. The Russian ship company, which lowered the price of tickets, is largely responsible for this influx. The Journey from Odessa to Jaffa now (1914) costs some fourteen rubles in all.

Accordingly every ship brings a large number of young people, for whom work must be found in the city or the colony, and the energetic B. who is at the head of the Labor Bureau has his hands full.

The Labor Bureau serves also as post-office for the workingmen. A large number of them receive their letters at the address of the Bureau. B. tells me that it is not always an easy matter to discover the addressee. His experience has already made him an expert in postal puzzles. Such directions as "To be given to the Carpenter" or "For my Husband" are child's play to him. Last week, however, he received a letter with the following address: "To be delivered to the same".

I was interested to learn what percentage of the toilers who come to Palestine remain permanently. I discovered that the percentage was very small. Ordinarily they come in large numbers just before Passover, and scatter over the colonies. By day they work in the orange groves and in the vineyards, and at night they sing: "Yoh–Ha–Li–Li", and dance till they can no longer stand on the their feet. Or they go strolling over the hills and amidst the gardens, and are happy and joyous. Should they catch a touch of the fever, they welcome it as part of the game. After all this is Eretz Yisroel,the skies are beautiful, one is young and is celebrating the liberation from the distractedness or from the hum-drum pettiness of life in the old home.

Weeks and months go by. And the weaker element, who are in the majority, grow downcast, lose their courage, and one fine day resolve to leave. This one goes to America, the other to Africa, a third returns home.

They have failed to pass the test.

There remain only the purified, the resolute, the thoroughly tested ones—the fighters and pioneers. They sink their roots into the soil, and become the best and soundest elements of the settlement.

TYPES

The number of students at the Gymnasium is increasing. Every class has been compelled to open parallel classes and some have had to open two. There are students here from every part of Europe, the United States, South America, Africa, and there was one even from Spain. Meanwhile almost every day, brings its share of newcomers, some of them tourists some to settle here for pleasure and rest, and others to do business. Wherever one turns one sees new houses going up. On every street one meets camels laden with building material and asses carrying on each side sacks filled with sand. No sooner is a house completed than it is rented, and rooms are very high.

We went out hunting for a home, and found it an impossible task. G. had reccommended to us an old Petrograd business man, who was now living on his rents—a fellow who had once written a book with the name *Waw ha-Mehappek* (the *waw* consecutive), and had published it at his own expense. Now he was going about with marvellous plans for extracting chemicals from sea-shells.

Since the old Jew lived alone with his wife, and had a home as spacious as a forest, perhaps we could rent two rooms from him at a reasonable price—at least, so said our friend G.

I understood that the man was doing a good business here, and I could not quite satisfy myself as to whether his praises were the result of his monopoly in hinges, or whether his profits were the just reward of his Zionism.

Later I learned that the Connecticut "builder" of the new settlement and the agent for American hinges employed only Arab labor on his buildings. Jewish workingmen were too radical—too radical to work for starvation wages.

For himself the Connecticut builder has erected a beautiful two-story structure, not far from the Gymnasium. Over the door, in large, golden letters, is inscribed the verse from Isaiah: "And they shall build houses and dwell therein". With genuine American modesty he omitted to mention the name of the builder that Isaiah had in mind.

On account of his great hurry to accomplish the first half of the verse some of the structures he was putting up collapsed before the second half of the verse could be fulfilled.

WIND-MILLS

My young acquaintance, the High School student of the eighth class, who is my bureau of information on everything, tells me that I must be sure to meet old Michael Halperin. That fellow—he assures me—is one of the most remarkable types to be found in Eretz Yisroel. To be in Tel-Aviv and not see Michael Halperin is an even greater shame than to be in Rome and not to see the pope.

Michael Halperin was born in Wilna. His father was a usurer, a Shylock, who was known in the entire district for his frightful stinginess. When the miser died, he left a fortune of several hundred thousand rubles to his only son and heir.

And herewith begins Michael's checkered, romantic career.

First of all the miser's son commenced to live in grand style, kept a double span of horses, plenty of servants, and lived like a lord.

After he had his fill of a high old time, he began to plan all manner of enterprises which he never carried out. Among these plans was that of issuing a gigantic talmudic encyclopedia. Later he journeyed to Eretz Yisroel, founded a factory in partnership with another, and in a very short time squandered a large sum of money. It is told, of this same period, that he once led a strike of the workingmen against his own establishment. Having got rid of the factory, he returned to Russia, and plunged heart and soul into the "Self-Defence", the S. S., and other radical movements.

After ten or twelve years of this he yearned once again for Palestine, whither he journeyed for the second time.

By that time, nothing was left him of all his inheritance, and he had to support himself and his family on his wages as a Shomer (watchman). But when funds were collected for the young Turks, and Michael Halperin hadn't even a mutilated "Kabak" between him and starvation, Michael Halperin removed his Russian boots, and presented them to the Turkish revolution, and walked home barefoot.

A couple of years ago he sent to a Jewish daily in New York "an open letter", in which he appealed to the Jewish nation for the sum of fifteen million dollars. For the aforesaid sum he guaranteed to bring over a million Jews out of exile and settle them in Palestine. And should he fail to carry out this project, he promised to administer his own punishment, declaring to the world's Jewry that he would shoot himself.

Once he took up a position on the streets of Jaffa, sword in hand, and began to yell: "We must capture our land, once and for all. Things must come to an end '.

And on the very spot, so as to show that he was ready to do his part and would let nothing daunt him, he struck himself a blow with the sword and almost severed his arm.

This exploit cost him many weeks in the hospital, but it did not dampen his enthusiasm in the slightest degree.

After hearing such tales as these I was eager to meet the old fellow, and I begged my student acquaintance to introduce me to him as soon as possible.

One day, as I stood leaning against the stone veranda of our boarding-house, I was approached by a man of about fifty-five, with white hair that straggled over his shoulders, a flowing white beard, and small, good-natured eyes that smiled with a child-like expression. He wore a loose, white smock with a broad, leather belt, and a coarse felt hat. From a distance one might have taken him for Tolstoi. He comes closer to me.

"Shalom!"

He stretches out his hand in a warm greeting:

"I am Michael Halperin."

I hesitate to remind him of his article in the New York paper. I tell myself that he has surely long ago forgotten it, that he must be ashamed of it. So I speak but half words, beat about the bush, and am afraid to come to the point.

However, he spares me all these diplomatic tricks; he himself launches at once into a discussion of the self-same plan in which he still has the same firm faith as he had at the time he addressed an open letter to the Jewry of the world. The plan is as clear as day. "Skotovodstvo" (cattle-breeding). The Jews must take to "Skotovodstvo". "Skotovodstvo" requires hardly any money. "Skotovodstvo" multiplies beyond count in a very short time, and so on. "Skotovodstvo" would build up the Jewish nation and would achieve the redemption. We must become Bedouins.

I see that "Skotovodstvo" is a favorite term of his.

The "idealists"—he proclaims, heatedly—are the only ones that have accomplished anything. Moses, Christ, Muhammed, Loyola (he employed the last name with emphasis), were the only ones who had ever achieved great results. The "realists" had never done a thing in their lives. "We must conquer the land by might. We must wage war with sword and bow. Ahad Ha'am's 'Spiritual centre' leads to nothing. We must fight—" and his fists clench.

As he speaks, his good-natured eyes smile, as if to say: "Dont pay any attention to him. He is really a soft-hearted, peaceable fellow."

He tells me that at the time of the first revolution of the young Turks he assembled a Jewish company which was to have charge of the city's defence, taking the place of the soldiers in the Jaffa garrison, who would thus be released to march against Constantinople.

But the revolution was over before matters got that far. All that remains of this exploit is a picture in which he was photographed together with other Turkish officers, and under his name is the inscription: "Capitan de la brigade Juive".

My kodak began to call me: Take a snapshot of the captain of the Jewish brigade. I could not resist the temptation.

He consented, but on condition that I should never reproduce it in a newspaper or use it for any other purpose of publicity. But in the childish eyes of the "captain" lurked the hidden hope that I should break my promise.

Out came my kodak, and we stepped down from the veranda. He took up a pose not far from the house, and at once the sun flooded him from head to foot. I focussed the camera, looked into the finder, and saw the old fellow smiling good-naturedly into his mustache. I pressed the lever and congratulated myself on my successful bit of work.

A few days later, when I had the film developed, it was seen that fate had protected the captain's modesty better than he himself. Instead of Michael Halperin there appeared a strip of Russian shirt and a hazy spot that should have been a head.

In the course of the year that I spent in Eretz Yisroel I met other members of Don Quixote's tribe.

One of them, a colonist from Gedara, a Jew in his seventies, came to Rehoboth for the express purpose of seeing me, because—he said—he had heard that I had translated the Bible into "Jargon". Wherefore he had come to tell me that he himself, many years ago, had translated the song of *Haazinu* (Give ear, ye heavens).

We get into conversation. In one breath he lets me know that is he a grandson of the "Shakh,"* that he has a large household in Gedara, and that despite his age he toils in the fields together with his farmhands. He stretches out his arm and asks me to feel it. I comply with his request: muscles as tough as iron.

*A celebrated commentator on the Shulhan 'Aruk

He smiles:

"I am a man of seventy. And just as you see me, I can plough a whole field without any assistance."

Has he any children?

"Yes, a son"—and his smile vanishes. He must not appear in the colony. He is at Galilee. There was a fight between Jews and Arabs. An Arab attacked him. His son is a giant of a chap, and struck the Arab a strong blow, meant only to draw blood; but the blow proved fatal.

After that the Arabs and the Jews made peace. The Arabs know the old man very well. Together with the family of the slain man they slaughtered a sheep, and ate the meat, but should his son appear, nobody could be sure that one of the slain man's relatives would not seek vengeance for the blood that had been shed. One of his laborers is an Arab, a relative of the murdered man. Whenever the old man is left alone in the field with him, he can see a sinister glint light up in the Arab's eyes, and he has to hasten away.

As we continue our conversation we come to the important point.

For years and years he has been going around with a plan to fill in part of the Mediterranean Sea and turn it into arable land. He intends to leave a certain sum in his will for that purpose, a sum to be deposited until capital and interest shall have grown to such a vast amount that the work may be begun.

To my question, why fill in part of the sea, when three-quarters of the land is lying fallow, he would not even listen. The more land the better.

A LETTER

Dear. . . . .

In order to understand it, one must be in Eretz Yisroel. And perhaps it is impossible, and even unnecessary to *understand*. One feels it in the air, in one's veins, in one's muscles, and in every heart-beat.

All those puzzling queries to which one expected to find an answer here—are not answered here. Only you wake up one morning and the whole band of dark thoughts has disappeared. They have all vanished overnight, like a ghastly nightmare, and not a trace of them has remained. You can hardly believe it. You suspect that they are lurking somewhere. And you seek everywhere for them, being hardly able to recall what they looked like. No longer do you seek an interpretation of your interrupted dream. You behold the firm, clear reality all about you, and you doubt whether you ever really had such a dream.

Eretz Yisroel has its own logic, just as every great faith has its own logic. Ordinary logic is of no avail here. You will accomplish nothing with it.

That dark, leaden cloud which hung over your spirit, weakening and disheartening, is quickly dissipated by the clear sun of Eretz Yisroel.

Only now that I am in Eretz Yisroel and my soul feels secure about the future, do I begin to understand how many heavy stones weighed upon my heart in the Goluth. Now for the first time do I see what effort was necessary in order to bring myself to *believe*, in order not to be dragged down into the slough of despondence.

A bridge of cobwebs over an abyss, and the abyss drawing and calling.

...Eretz Yisroel is the chief concern, the centre of all things. In the Hebrew High School all subjects are taught from the standpoint of Eretz Yisroel. In geography, Palestine is taken as the homeland of the students, and indeed the central point from which all other lands must be studied.

There are students here from Russia and from other countries who have come merely to finish their education and then to return to their native land. And yet they have developed the same conception of Eretz Yisroel, as the central point of all the countries. The other lands are foreign countries.

Have not their fathers, dwelling in the snowy lands of the north, prayed for rain after the feast of Tabernacles, and dew after Passover, because such is the prayer in sub-tropical Eretz Yisroel? With their fathers it was a prayer, automatically repeated, and a yearning; with their children it is a living conviction and a spirited determination.

I go out into the street and look deep into the eyes of the Jews who happen to pass by; I watch their gait, their raised heads, their speech, their motions, and I discern that a change has come over them. I sense in them a certain something that I have never noticed in any Jew of any land in the world.

This has been breathed into them by the air of Eretz Yisroel; it has come to them with their first footstep upon the soil that their forefathers inhabited. This self-same soil has been awaiting their footsteps for hundreds of years, and no sooner did they touch the ground than hidden sap gushed forth from the depths and streamed into them, fructifying their souls and strengthening their hearts. Whereupon their backs straightened as if by magic, their eyes were filled with courage and dignity as if by miracle, and their hands and limbs became freer, surer.

People and land have come together, and the meeting of the long-parted twins has been as spontaneous and impetuous as the attraction of chemical affinities.

You dwell now, and up to a few months ago I dwelt in a land where Jews are free, very free, and rich, very rich. We both witnessed our brethern acting in unrestricted freedom in the greatest city in America. And we beamed to see, in the street-cars and in the subways of New York, Jews seated with Jewish newspapers spread out before them, as if they were in their own homes.

But the expression that their eyes have in Eretz Yisroel never shone from them *there*. In Eretz Yisroel their eyes have altogether stopped turning about and asking: "What will people say?" Here we have a Judaism that lives in and of itself, and feels that it owes nobody but itself an account—a Judaism that is stretching its limbs and preparing for great deeds.

No, you are wrong. I am not blinded: not everybody that comes to Eretz Yisroel is a hero and an idealist. But this is not at all important. Let many come, multitudes of them. Time presses, and we can't afford to be too exacting. The good are often slow-footed. We need chiefly numbers, quantity. We are little concerned with quality. For my part, let them be horse-thieves. The horse-thief's grandfather was an upright Jew, and the horse-thief's son or grandchild will be a sound, worthy citizen of Eretz Yisroel.

Whenever I meet one of those petty souls who have come here to the settlement in quest of a field for their sordid interests—the kind that stand upon the shoulders of the nation in order to be taken for the head; or whenever I meet one of those speculators who increase the cost of the land and pretend to be builders and pioneers (who have Zion on their lips and the golden calf in their hearts), EretzYisroel is not a jot the lower in my affection. Such persons will not pollute or desecrate Eretz Yisroel. Rather will Eretz Yisroel cleanse and purify them, or if not them, those that will issue from their loins.

These are the decaying seeds from which will spring forth sound, full-laden stalks.

Behind each of these petty, ugly souls I behold a lurking shadow. It is the shadow of one that will "inherit the land and dwell therein."

See, for example, how in America there have grown up "Zeligs" and "gyp the bloods", types that our race has never known. And in this way America has cleansed the Jewish nation. For every millionaire, a "gangster"; for every judge, a white-slaver.

And this is what took place in Eretz Yisroel:

A young man, the son of wealthy parents who lived in a large Russian city, strayed into evil ways. He began to chum with vagabonds and rogues until he himself became a thief and a thug of the worst sort. All at once he takes it into his head to see what Eretz Yisroel is like. The semi-Bedouin life of the Shomerim appeals to his wild, restless nature. He is a good marksman, and rides like the devil incarnate. So he offers his services to the *ha-Shomer*, and is accepted.

Now he is one of the most devoted and most idealistic youths in that heroic group.

Eretz Yisroel has redeemed him.

In Eretz Yisroel all Judaism will find its redemption. The joy and the light of the Torah and the Prophets has become dimmed by terror and pictures of death, and covered by a thick cobweb of melancholy. Because the Jews wandered about in exile, and the Shekinah wandered with them, the light and the gladness of former Jewish life were defiled. A perpetual light, however, flickered, barely snatching from the surrounding darkness a tiny corner near the Holy Ark. Now it will become a vast sun. Jewish sunniness and Jewish joy will find their redemption.

The source of dejection is weakness; the source of happiness is strength. Now we shall become strong, and our life will become one great joy.

How much energy shall now flow into us! For the greatest part of it used to go to waste in erecting ghetto-walls. Our mightiest men had to become guards and watch over the gates, lest someone should steal in over night or someone of us steal out. Now all this energy will be released to build up new Tel-Avivs, to plant orange groves, develop Jewish industries, and found Jewish universities.

Our anchor will no longer be in the past, but in the future. No longer "in the name of and for the glory of our ancestors," but "in the name of our children's children."

You will never understand it all, for it was not made to be *understood*. Come hither, and all at once everything will grow clear to you, and bright as the light of the seven days. Bring with you but a single thing: love, or at least the will to love.

Hate shuts up, and you may come here and leave just as you came. And perhaps you will even take with you accumulated interest on the principle of hate or dissatisfaction and fault-finding that you brought along.

And just one word more: This is the great beginning. The first corner-stones are being laid. Come, let us, like little children, stand and watch the building of a house. Yonder where you are everything is already done, or almost done.

Your . . . .

A CHANGE OF RESIDENCE

Our friend G. was very desirous of having us remain in Tel-Aviv. He felt sure that even if we did settle in some colony, we should not be able to stay there long. We would miss the city life and would return to *bustling* Tel-Aviv. But not even the worst prognostications could alter our determination to leave the town. We yearned for a quiet, peaceful nook.

The doors and the windows of our boarding-house were almost always open. Promptly at day-break barefoot Shloyme would open them, and not until late at night would he close them. There was very little difference between outdoors and inside. The people, I began to think, were the same way: door and gate wide open, just like a public thoroughfare. No intimate corners, no deep inner life, no moods. The conversation generally turned upon the Gymnasium, the school for girls, the Anglo-Palestine-Bank, the Planters' League, colonization, and yet again colonization.

The entire population lived more in the streets and on the verandas than in their homes. In my room I could hear the din and the shrill chatter of the street. And there was not a spot where one might find seclusion.

The streets of the town are short and few in number. If you go out for a walk you are forever encountering the same persons. Once I made it a point to keep count. In the course of some thirty minutes I met and greeted a certain instructor, an acquaintance of mine, a dozen times. He loomed up before me at every street corner. The last time we came across each other we both felt embarrassed.

Grass and flowers were few. The saplings, which bordered the street and were hedged about with protective boards, were rather stuck than grown into the soil. Everything was new, built upon sand; nowhere was there a trace of anything which had taken deep root.

Sometimes Tel-Aviv appeared to me a large, beautiful station, and the light—the naked, shrieking light—disturbed and provoked me.

In the meantime, in the surrounding orchards the dark-green branches were besprinkled with white. Alongside of the last golden orange the new blossoms wafted their fragrance, and their odor became daily more piquant and sweet. A warm breeze carried the fragrance out of the orchards into Tel-Aviv, and from Tel-Aviv out into the sea.

Later—they say—when all the flowers are in bloom, the sailors on ships, who are miles away from the shore, can smell the fragrance of the blossoms. The odor of the orange blossoms got into my blood. I wanted to be surrounded by a multitude of orange-blossoms, undisturbed peace, and boundless verdure.

We had some time before made the acquaintance of S., one of the pioneer colonists of Rehoboth, who is known in both Hebrew and Yiddish literature for his sketches of the new settlement, and even more for his little tales of Arab life, under the name Khawaja Musa. Khawaja means Mr, or Master, and Musa is the Arabic for Moses. So that his Arab employes call him Khawaja Musa. Whence his pen-name. He is a man of about forty-odd years, of medium build, solid, with a round florid face framed in a sparse black beard, small, dreamy eyes, and a deep reservoir of hidden energy.

At that time, together with many other prominent colonists, he was involved in a murder trial that had grown out of a clash between the Jews of Rehoboth and the Arabs of the village of Zarnuka, in which a Jew and an Arab had been shot.

The Arabs of Zarnuka had always lived in peace with their Jewish neighbors, and, besides this, they made a living in Rehoboth, where they were employed and where they sold their products. The sheikh Abu-Halib intervened, the feud was allayed, and peace reigned once more.

The affair, however, was already in the hands of the Government, and both sides were quivering with anxiety to tear themselves free from the talons of Turkish "justice". Poor Zarnuka became even poorer, and the matter cost the community of Rehoboth a little fortune, in addition to the fact that for a time it crippled all the communal labors of the colony.

S. had to hide from the Turkish officers, and his visits to Jaffa were made secretly. He visited us several times at the boarding-house, and we became very close friends. He advised us to come and settle in

Rehoboth, the most beautiful, most flourishing colony in Judea.

That Rehoboth really is the most beautiful and at the same time the most progressive colony in the entire settlement was the opinion not only of Khawaja Musa, who had devoted his best years to its construction, but also that of everybody to whom we mentioned the subject.

F. was very enthusiastic over Rehoboth. He planned to build his own home there. Indeed he had already negotiated about a piece of land for that purpose. His intention was to erect for himself a home there, with a garden near by, and live and create in peaceful seclusion. The remarkable thing about it all is, that despite all his dreams of seclusion, one fine day, almost without taking leave of anybody, he journeyed off to Berlin to become the editor of a new Hebrew journal.

We decided to go to Rehoboth.

S. was notified that we were coming by the Jaffa-Jerusalem railroad to Ramleh, and that he should send a conveyance to receive us. It was hard to part with our new friends. But there was the hope that we would visit Tel-Aviv from time to time.

When we reached Ramleh we were surrounded by half-a-dozen ragged, barefoot Arabs. Each of them tried to snatch our valises from our hands. These were donkey-drivers who offered to take us to Rehoboth. I waited and looked in every direction for S.'s man. Nowhere was he to be seen or heard. Apart from the fact that I did not care to entrust myself to the tender mercies of these donkey-drivers, I had never ridden anything, except in my earliest days of childhood upon a broom-stick. I was therefore not at all desirous of being initiated into that art in Ramleh.

It occurred to me that perhaps one of these donkey-drivers has been sent by Hawaja Musa, who, during the twenty-five years that he has been living in Eretz Yisroel, has forgotten that one may love Eretz Yisroel and yet detest donkeys. So I waved my arms and gave these fellows to understand, in their own eloquent deaf-and-dumb language, that I was waiting for a note from Hawaja Musa.

"A note? With the utmost respect!" cries an old white-bearded Arab, that is to say, so I interpret his words. And surely enough, he at once steps aside, and in a stealthy manner, so that I should not notice him, picks up a scrap of paper, which had a couple of words on them.

"Here is the note", and his mouth is ready to swear by the beard of the prophet that he speaks the truth.

I don't know how the story would have ended, had not the teamster Mahmud, whom S. had sent to meet us, suddenly appeared. With true Arab indifference he had been looking on from afar all this time, watching us being pulled in every direction, and had delayed his entrance until the fifth act.

For about an hour we journeyed over a sandy road. Upon Mahmud's invitation we crawled down from the wagon several times, and we thanked Allah that we were not required to help to push it along.

We were now within sight of Rehoboth. This is the limit of the mounted Jewish guards' patrol at night.

After a quarter of an hour our wagon stopped near the "Malon Klivitsky".

The Colony, framed-in orchards, lay peacefully basking in the spring sunshine. Few persons were on the streets, and everywhere hovered a healthful, contented peacefulness. I felt that here I would find that quiet nook I had been seeking, and that here I would build my nest.

REHOBOTH

For three days a steady rain fell. This was the beginning of the spring rains from which the soil of Palestine drinks its supply against the six months of drought, just as a camel fills itself with water in preparation for a journey across the desert. It has become warm and sunny once more, and all afternoon I have been sauntering about the colony.

I went as far as Jaffa Street and entered a long avenue planted on either side with eucalyptus and mimosa, which the Arabs call "Shajarel-Yahud" (the Jewish trees). Before the new Jewish settlement came, these species had never been seen in these parts.

Near the avenue, in the shadow of a tree, sat a group of little girls playing. They had all been born in Rehoboth, and were bright, healthy creatures. Their little faces were tanned by the sun, and they had black, genuine Jewish eyes. Out of their eyes laughed the joy of life and the self-confidence of a rejuvenated people.

"Shalom, Yeladot!"

"Shalom, Adoni!"

They looked at me half-embarrassed and half-inquisitively. I drew nearer and began a conversation with them. Of course, they all spoke Hebrew. That is the mother-tongue of the Rehoboth children. From their childish lips it sounds beautiful, and, I would say, even musical, and so natural withal, that every argument against the artificial revival of a language disappears of itself as soon as you hear them talk.

During the course of our chat a girl of nine made the confident statement that there were more Jews in Eretz Yisroel than in all the other countries of the world put together.

A companion of about ten, with a head of black hair cut short like a boy's and with smart, wide-awake eyes, was not entirely in agreement. "More than all the other countries —yes" she said: "but not more than Russia. There are more Jews there than in Eretz Yisroel."

"About how many more?" I was curious to know.

For a moment the childish forehead was knitted in thought, and her black brows contracted. Her brain was evidently hard at work.

"Twice as many as in Eretz Yisroel", came the answer at length.

"And in America?"—I continued.

"In America?" they all laugh, in concert, and their sound, white teeth glitter in the sunlight. "In America there most certainly are not as many Jews as there are in Eretz Yisroel."

And I thought: after all, perhaps the little girls are right.

Many Jews, who supposedly live in Russia and in America, have their souls in Palestine.

As soon as I had stepped a few paces away from them, they took each other's hands and formed a circle. And a tiny tot strode around the circle and sang the child's song: "I am going to the fields."

A narrow path brought me to a small hill. This hillock is a favorite spot with the young folks, and has already been crowned with the name of Giv'at ha-Ahavah (Lovers' Hill). The beautiful flowers that grow upon Lovers' Hill as well as their neighbors round about are naturally very secretive. But among themselves they have many an ardent secret to tell.

I paused on the top of the hill. My glances made rapid rounds of the landscape, not knowing whither to turn first.

To the west, below in the valley, lay the dark green orange groves and almond orchards, drinking in the golden flood of sunshine. Among the gardens and behind them were scattered vegetable patches and meadows, revealing every shade of green. Far in the distance shimmered a yellow band, the sandy shore of the Mediterranean Sea.

On the other side, amidst a profusion of eucalypti, cedars, cypresses, and mulberry-bushes, stood the self-important colony in all its beauty, with its white kalsomined houses and their red roofs. Every house, neat and pretty, reflected the warm rays, and behind and above the houses, resting its back against the blue mist of the mountain of Judah, rose the simply constructed synagoogue with its large, semi-circular windows.

"And it shall come to pass in the end of days, that the mountain of the Lord's house shall be established as the top of the mountains, and shall be exalted above the hills... And many people shall go and say: Come ye,and let us go up to the mountain of the Lord,to the house of the God of Jacob; and He will teach us of His ways, and we will walk in His paths...."

Who could have whispered these verses into my ear?

Gazing upon the soft, dreamy hills of Judea as they swam in a sea of mist, I thought that "mountain" was too corporeal, too work-a-day a name. Perhaps "soul of a mountain" would be better? If mountains die and have a world beyond this one, they must look like the hills of Judea.

There they lie beneath their veil of mist, day and night, dreaming. The sun rises and sets, the stars twinkle and go out, and the mountains lie wrapped in their blue keffiah and dream on. Memories? Hopes? All at once, unseen of an eye, unheard of an ear, it seemed as if vast flocks of winged dreams, which have been fluttering about for thousands of years, have begun to stir in quest of embodiment. A moment more and a shrill ram's horn will blare forth from somewhere and all at once every dream will become a flesh-and-blood reality, will take definite shape, and the "fields will begin to sing."

In the meantime the sun sank lower and lower. In the branches the birds have begun to trill with loud ecstasy, just as if they would like to sing their utmost before the cool night hushes their voices.

And now the lower edge of the vast red sun has touched the rim of the earth. The burial-hill of "Nebi Gendi" stands out in ever clearer outline against the western sky. Slowly the fiery ball disappears. And

now begins the genuine Eretz Yisroel sunset. Half the
sky is afire, and from moment to moment the con-
flagration rises. Behind the sandy sea-shore lies the sun
like an invisible sorcerer, every moment revealing a
new wonder of color.

A cool evening breeze began to blow from the direction of the sea, and the twilight was saturated with
the passionate, sweet odor of the orange-trees in full
bloom. I descended the hill and returned to the colony.
Once more I strolled through the avenue of eucalypti
and mimosae.

A caravan of camels came along the road from the
town. The camels' necks rose and fell rythmically
and the bells on their necks tinkled in the evening air
like the echo of a distant dream.

An old white-bearded Arab, with the countenence
of a desert prophet and with big, dirty feet, passed by
on a small donkey. He rode along in leisurely fashion
as if he had a thousand years in which to make his
journey.

From the vineyards came the wail of the hungry
jackals. First one, then two; and the cries grew more
frequent, and more joined in the chorus each time.

I raised my eyes to the east and beheld a huge, wax-
colored moon, clambering hurriedly up from behind
the synagogue in pursuit of the sun's place, and in keen
race with it.

Half of the sky was drenched in the red, yellow, and
greenish colors of the sun, and in the other half the
moon was trying to outdo its rival in the west.

The colony lay nestling amidst its trees, and in the silence drank down the intoxicating odor of the oranges, as it thrilled with delight at the rivalry between the sun and the moon, which seemed to contend for its favor.

METAMORPHOSES

In one corner of the vacant lot directly opposite our inn, on a little hill, stands a wooden shack with a tiny window in front.

From that shack and through that tiny window are distributed every evening, by the light of a small lamp, the letters that come from Jaffa.

The mail is first brought to the "postmaster," an old bachelor who takes his unsalaried office very seriously. Only after he has sorted the mail, is it delivered into the hands of a paid assistant whose duty it is to bring them into this shack and distribute them.

This assistant works all day long in an orchard. When he returns from work he sets enthusiastically about the cultivation of his own garden of vegetables, which he hopes will in time make him a rich man. There is still an idle hour left in the evening, and since it is a pity to waste it, he employs it as the distributor of the mail.

About eight o'clock the knoll about the shack resounds with the voices of Jewish maidens dressed in white and of Jewish youths in girdled smocks.

They stand and wait for the little window to open. In the meantime they chat and laugh at the top of their voices, scrutinizing each other in the darkness. And class-conscious workingmen invite the daughters of the "Boazes"* to a stroll.

* Such is the name given by the workingmen in Eretz Yisroel to a colonist who does not work himself, after Boaz of the Book of Ruth.

In the midst of it all a black-eyed maiden begins some sort of Hebrew song, and as the chorus chimes in, the mail is altogether forgotten.

A few paces from the mail-shack stand two tall poles. Across the poles, horizontally, lies a beam, and from the beam hangs a bell, with a rope trailing from it.

Five times a day there comes one of our Yemenite kin— a fellow with long, curly ear-locks, and bare, chocolate-colored feet—to pull that bell. The bell begins to toll so loud that the most distant orchards echo with its ringing.

The bell sounds for the first time very early in the morning, when the dew is still upon the grape vine, and from every direction of the colony there begin to appear workingmen with queer, broad straw hats upon their heads and queer, large baskets in their hands.

The size of the basket is more for effect than for use, for it generally contains not more than a bread-slice of crepuscular color, which is to say, neither white nor black. Together with the bread lies a huge, white-bellied cucumber, and, if God is kind, a slice of cheese.

The bell rings for the second time at half-past eleven. And when its shrill clang is heard, one knows that in the shade of the orange or almond trees sit young Jewish people at their ease, eating bread and green cucumber, taking their pleasure in the land that flows with milk and honey.

At half-past twelve it rings again: "Enough carousing, boys. Back to work." Whereupon they return to their hoes.

The bell sounds for the fourth time at half-past five in the evening. Once again the queer, broad-brimmed straw hats appear, and together with them the queerly huge straw baskets—this time as empty as a house after the pre-Passover cleaning.

In the meantime night falls. The *diligence* from Jaffa has arrived long since, and unloaded the passengers together with their bundles and trunks of all sorts, near Padua's grocery. The old Jew with the white goatee, who distributes the daily *Ha-Herut* as soon as it arrives with the coach, is already seated in the synagogue poring over his chapter of the Mishnah.

From the club of the "Poalim" comes the sound of songs in every scale. After a day's digging in Jewish vineyards, and after the royal supper of tea and bread, they sing: "El Yivneh ha-Galil" (May the Lord build up Galilee).

And in the midst of this comes the ding-dong, ding-dong once again.

This time the bell is ringing as a signal for Shomerim to commence their silent duty, so that the thousands of souls of the colony may be able to sleep in security, knowing that "neither sleeps nor slumbers the guard of Israel."

Besides this schedule of five daily ringings, the bell summons the residents of the settlement to the annual assembly when the head of the community is elected, or to other important gatherings. If the bell is heard to ring at other times, by day or by night, then people know that something had happened in some orchard or other. Whereupon the young men seize their rifles and dash forth, while the old folk tremble apprehensively.

Later I learned that the bell was a church bell, a worn-out church bell, which the head of the community had purchased and converted to Jewish purposes. This explains why the bell often doesn't work right, and why it happens that when it is supposed to ring twice it adds another ring, half tinkle and half groan. At any rate this is more reasonable an explanation than that offered me by an acquaintance, who said that the Temoni who pulls the bell doesn't know his business. The matter is simple: the bell was not entirely converted. It longs for the church.

Eretz Yisroel in general is a wonderful place for conversion, and for giving non-Jewish things the benefit of a rather queer Judaization. Take for example the songs that are sung here—and there is a great deal of singing done here. One may hear tunes from every nation and language. If you draw nearer and make out the words, you discover that they have taken a Russian, German, English, French, or American tune and yoked it to a Hebrew song. A few days ago I heard some tots singing "Yankee Doodle". Upon closer investigation it appeared that they were singing to the tune of "Yankee Doodle" the Hebrew school-song, "Hinneh kakhah ve-hinneh kakhah".

On the other hand, in Ekron, a pious, old-fashioned colony, they have converted a genuinely Jewish institution into a place for work-a-day uses. When I was there not long ago, an elderly colonist took me along to show me the former Mikvah which had been transformed into a dairy, the products of which are sent daily *via* Ramleh to Jaffa. One could see that even the old stones of the Mikvah which had been built with Baron de Rothschild's money and by the Baron's representatives, swelled with pride at their new function and at the white cans bought by the colonists themselves with their own hard-earned money.

In this same Ekron, while strolling through the street, I noticed a little garden of flowers near a house. I paused to look at it and felt it my duty to discover the Hebrew name for each different flower.

Some children were standing close by. I asked them. They knew no more than I did. So I turned to a little girl of fourteen or fifteen who happened at the moment to thrust her head out of a near-by window. Her answer was curt and sharp:

"Ain Shemot la-Perahim" (Flowers have no names).

But flowers do have names in Eretz Yisroel. And some of the names are quite piquant. Thus pansies are called in Hebrew "Amnon and Tamar".

However, names or no names, flowers grow unbidden in Eretz Yisroel. They were wont to bloom when not a soul was here, and the difficulty in finding a name for them will by no means prevent them from continuing to flourish. And it seems to me that the fairest flowers that grow in Eretz Yisroel are precisely those which nobody has planted and nobody has given any thought to.

There is no sight more refreshing than the fields which, in the months of February and March, are literally covered with every kind of flower. They grow without any outside effort, without the ministrations of a watering pot, and without the aid of a beneficent gardner. I have never seen their like in any garden, and they seem to invite you: "Take, dear friend; pluck as many as you please, for there are plenty here, thank God, for you and for thousands of others. Soon the hot days will come, and we will disappear altogether."

I am attracted especially by the red anemones—the rose of the valley mentioned in the Song of Songs—and by the yellow daisies. So I pluck one of each kind, and stick it in my buttonhole. The combination of the two colors fascinates me. To be sure, they do not last long, but I can afford the luxury of replacing them frequently.

COUNTRYMEN

Shortly after my arrival in Rehoboth Khawaja Musa introduced me to a "countryman" of mine—a young man by the name of M., with blue, naive eyes, and bashful, almost girlish, manners. In New York, where he would undoubtedly have been minus a beard or mustache, it would at once have been plain that he was still very young. Here, however, an experienced eye must first imagine him without a beard in order to discover his age.

I learn that at the age of fourteen this reserved M. had been seized with the *wanderlust*. So he forsook his little village in Russia, and set forth into the wide world alone. He even wandered as far as Cape Town, Africa. There he suffered all sorts of privations before working himself up to anything like a decent position. He did not care to remain there permanently, and longed for Jewish surroundings, so in a couple of years he left that place for America. During all the time that he spent in both these countries the former student had not ceased to improve his mind in his leisure hours. He bought a large number of English and Hebrew books, and devoted much time to reading and studying.

The heart of the quiet, bashful M. was always drawn away from the hubbub and commotion of American life.

"And besides this", he tells me, "wherever I went I saw that a Jew was hated even among the free nations.

I noticed this in the cars, in the streets, and everywhere. It stung me to the quick, and I felt as though I were choking. So I felt that Eretz Yisroel was the right place for me. Off I went to Rehoboth, purchased a parcel of land, and tilled it myself, and when, at the end of a hard day's work, I came back exhausted, I stretched myself out on the cold floor, and my weariness had the taste of Paradise. For I had grown weary digging *my* own, *our* soil."

Now M. is the proprietor of a large orchard. Outside of his passion for Eretz Yisroel, which he loves with body and soul, he is a fervent devotee of Emerson, who is always on his lips. He has even attempted to translate his essays into Hebrew. And even as great as his love for Eretz Yisroel and Emerson is his hatred of New York.

"Where can you find," he asks, after we have become a bit more intimate, "so many ignoramuses and so much bluff? Take for example", he continues, as if I personally were to blame, "your Yiddish newspapers."

And while we are talking he inconsistently extracts from his pocket an old Yiddish newspaper, and begins to read to me a feuilleton that he wrote when he was in New York—a description of the ocean.

M.'s father-in-law, Mr Z., is one of the richest inhabitants of the colony. He came here from Chicago, where, in the course of the several decades that he lived there, he built up a large wholesale grocery business. Z. was a maskil—a free-thinker, who yet was very fond of the Bible. The whole day he would be engrossed body and soul in his money-making, but as soon as he managed to get an hour to himself, it was his greatest pleasure to delve into the interpretation of a difficult verse in the Bible.

He had only one child, a girl, who had been brought up like all the Jewish daughters of well-to-do American parents. She had her High School and her chums while her father made money and burrowed into the Bible. But when the girl was graduated from High School, and the time came to think about finding her a husband, the Bible-studying grocer thrust aside his ledger, and began to take account of the situation. He could not bear the thought, he told me at our first meeting, that a grandchild of his should bear a name like Tom or Dick, when we had a Bible full of beautiful, gem-like names, and that only at the cost of great agony would it be possible to make him swallow a few spoonfuls of "biblical history".

So Z. sold his flourishing business, took his wife and his only daughter, journeyed to Eretz Yisroel, and settled in Rehoboth. Here he bought land, became the proprietor of an orange grove, and built himself a fine home with spacious verandas from which one may view the hills of Judea and the sands of the Mediterranean. Here the Bible studies of Z. have acquired an altogether different aspect. There is no better interpreter for a difficult chapter of the Bible than the hills of Judea, especially when viewed from Z.'s lofty balcony.

But the Bible was not enough to take up all the time of this small but energetic Chicago wholesaler. He was not accustomed to sitting idle. So he threw himself with his old enthusiasm into matters of public weal, helped instal a water-conduit system in the colony, put the postal system in order, and for a time served as postmaster. He busied himself very much with the improvement of the condition of the Yemenites, and in various ways took a leading part in the upbuilding of the settlement.

In the meantime the girl from Chicago learned to speak Hebrew fluently, and became to all intents and purposes a daughter of Rehoboth. The logical match then was: the New York youth who hated New York with the daughter of the Chicagoan who hated Chicago. In addition to this, perhaps Emerson and the Bible also had a share in bringing the two sides together.

Together with his wife, the former High School girl, M. began the study of books on horticulture, especially such as had to do with California, which is climatically similar to Eretz Yisroel. Many of the new horticultural methods with which M. had become acquainted in his studies he tried to put into immediate effect in his own orchard. The result of the experiment is as yet in doubt. Older colonists make a wry face.

Madame M., however, is far more successful with the flower-garden which she planted before her house, and which she tends personally. There are all sorts of specimens in this garden, and their young proprietress is very proud of them.

Not far from the house where Z. lives stands the beautiful villa of the pious Australian millionaire, who comes hither for a few months every year. He is a manufacturer, and his fortune is estimated at many millions. During the whole time of his visit he sits almost day and night studying the Talmud.

Behind his house he has had a *pardes* planted. I believe that the main trees there are of *Esrogim.* After a few years he will be able to pray in Sidney with "fruit of the goodly tree" sent to him from his own orchard in Eretz Yisroel. That is *his* sport. Many stories are told of his charity. Like a genuinely pious Jew he believes in anonymous donations. So whenever he comes to the synagogue to pray, he leaves on the reading-desk a couple of English sovereigns. But since there are not many persons in Rehoboth going around with English gold coins, the donor is readily discovered.

We had asked M.'s advice in regard to a place where we could live, and it turned out that he himself had a house that he could rent to us. The house was not really his, but it was as good as his. He was the overseer in charge of it. The house belonged to an American—a brother of his, in fact. His brother has a large furniture business in a small Pennsylvania town; he is doing very well, but he intends sooner or later to settle in Rehoboth. For that purpose he has already bought, through his brother in Eretz Yisroel, a house and a piece of land around it, and has had the land planted with every species of fruit tree.

In a few years the trees will have grown to full height and when the brother from Pennsylvania arrives with his family, he will find everything ready. The brother himself would be glad to come at once, for life out there has long been irksome to him, but his wife says that they must wait a few years till their children get through High School. So he's waiting, for the sake of domestic harmony.

The worry about an apartment had hung like a mill-stone around our necks, so that when we heard from M. that he had a suitable house for us, we were delighted. But very soon it appeared that our joy was somewhat premature.

The house really belongs to M.'s brother, and M. is to all intents and purposes the proprietor, but there is a tenant in the house, and the tenant refuses to move for any consideration. He likes the place. Moreover, he can't be blamed for being so fond if it. As M. says, the tenant is against paying rent, on principle, and when the rent is called for, his wife pours out a flood of vituperation. M. is a soft-hearted fellow. So he gets scared, and retreats from the enemy's camp, as speedily and as strategically as he can.

To make matters worse, this tenant is by trade a journeyman, painter and kalsominer. He says that M. must take the rent out in work. But suppose there is no work? He goes and puts on his apron, rolls up his sleeves, and paints his own shutters or whitewashes the walls. Well, after all the house is M.'s, so that he must pay for the painting and whitewashing anyway.

The score is even.   If only the fellow painted like a human being it would not be half so bad.   But he daubs on such crazy colors that they are enough to give one nausea.

M. is all helpless.   "Perhaps", he says, "we can manage the thing without harsh methods.   S. will take a hand in the matter, and the kalsominer will be made to listen to reason."

So we decide to remain at the inn until after Passover.

In the meantime we are the only guests at the hotel. There is no one to share with us its doubtful comforts, save now and then some transient traveller from Jaffa or from a near-by colony who is looked upon by the owner of the hotel as "better than nothing." The chief interest centres upon the tourists, who are watched for with popping eyes during the whole winter.   But they will not arrive for a few weeks yet. Between the tourist and the resident a great distinction is generally made in Eretz Yisroel.   The tourists themselves are divided into various categories; for example, Americans and those from other countries, such as bring along a great number of valises, and those with only one valise, and so on.

To dinner there come a couple of boarders who live elsewhere in the colony, and take their meals in the hotel. Near me sits an attractive young girl with small black eyes, long black lashes, and thick eyebrows, which almost meet over her well chiselled nose.   She comes from Odessa, where she attended the Gymnasium. She wished to become a teacher in one of the schools of Eretz Yisroel, and she is studying Hebrew diligently.

In the short time that she has been here she has achieved great results, and has already learned to be fairly fluent in—Yiddish. She has an uncle here. He is the white-haired old fellow that I see going by so often, dressed like a Polish overseer, in a short jacket, with trousers tucked into his high, polished riding-boots. He is an engineer from Odessa. It is rumored that he is rolling in wealth. Others add that he was once an apostate. He has purchased a piece of land in Rehoboth, and has planted it with castor-oil trees. He believes that Eretz Yisroel is in the future destined to become the chief source of supply of the purgative oil.

He is the one who "engineered" the stone stairway that leads to the hill on which the synagogue stands. The steps were originally made so that the older folk should find it easier to go to prayers. It has turned out, however, that it is easier for the older colonists to go by way of the hill than by the stone staircase. So the old folk climb laboriously up the old path while the young generation mount the new steps with long strides...

"DHUR 'L–KHAIL KHAMR"

To-day our hotel unexpectedly received exalted guests. The wife of the Pasha of Jerusalem arrived with two young ladies. All men were sent out of the hall until the Pasha's wife and her maids entered their room. At once there was a great commotion in the hotel, and ceaseless dashing to and fro. Every other moment brought a new order from the temporary harem. And since no man was permitted to set eyes upon them, the inn-keeper's young wife had to bring in to them the full bottles of beer, and take out the empty ones. Of course, all this was at the expense of the colony.

It was not until the next day that we were able to catch a glimpse of the guests, when the three women were already seated upon the hired carriage, ready to leave. The Pasha's wife, a young Turkish woman, wore a white, transparent yashmak, behind which one could make out clearly a white, round face. Behind the yashmak burned a pair of deep black eyes, with long, pencilled eyelashes. The faces of her companions were uncovered. One of them was a Sephardic young woman, the wife of the advocate Maial; she looked more Arab than Jewish. The other was a beautiful young Turkish maiden, who, as we later learned at the hotel, had returned not long before from France, where she had been reared. Both were dressed in the height of European fashion.

In honor of the guests, the leading Arabs of the surrounding villages rode over to the hotel, and gave a
"fantasia" in the front of the place, displaying every
sort of trick on their swift Arabian steeds. They flew
like a cyclone, each seeking to outdistance the other,
and in the midst of their gallop they would turn so
suddenly that it seemed as if at any moment horse and
rider would topple over. Others, at the height of the
race, would bend down close to the ground to pick up
something that lay there.

Most eager of all was a gray-haired old sheikh, with
a large white turban on his head. It seemed as if he
were actually glued to the saddle. The jockeys of
Sheepshead Bay would have burst with envy to see
that snow-white rider.

Late in the evening, as we sit in the quiet dining-
room and scent the strong fragrance of the orange-
blossoms striking against the window panes, a horse-
man stops before the inn. The door opens, and in
comes a slender young Bedouin. He wears a loose,
black "abaye" buckled tight at the neck. A broad,
white "keffiah" secured around his head by a thick
black "agal" hangs down upon his shoulder. Around
his waist is a cartridge belt. At his side, a Browning.
On his boots, clinking spurs.

He orders something to eat. In the meantime we
strike up an acquaintance, and it turns out that the
Bedouin speaks a fair Hebrew, a bad Yiddish, and a
very good Russian. His father has an orange grove
half-way between Rehoboth and Vadi-Khanin. They

live among the Arabs, and get along very well with them. The Arabs are excellent people, only you must know how to deal with them. And *he* knows how, so that they are the best of friends. It was from an Arab friend that he bought his horse, which he wouldn't exchange for anything in the world. To tell the exact truth, he had purchased but one leg. Three of the horse's legs still belonged to the previous owner.

"Only one leg?"

He smiles compassionately at my hopeless ignorance, and explains to me that not on his life would an Arab sell a mare without making the condition that one or more of the colts shall belong to him. Three legs meant three colts. First the previous owner takes his share; only then comes the purchaser's turn. From the praise of his horse he proceeds to the topic of riding in general. There is nothing in the world that can compare with abandoning yourself to a wild gallop. With good reason do the Arabs say: "Dhur l-khail Khamr", (the back of a horse is wine).

He never uses the *diligence*. That's all right for old folks and women. And he likes best to ride by night. Fear of an attack? Let the other fellow be afraid of him. He and a young friend of his recently wanted to have some fun, so they made a sham attack upon a caravan of Arab camel-drivers. There was a commotion, and the drivers ran off in terror, leaving their camels behind. Whereupon he and his companion rode off and were much delighted with their Bedouin trick.

He comes to Rehoboth for the mail (and perhaps for the good looking girls near the post-office). And so he dropped in to get a bite.

Perhaps we'll pay their *pardes* a visit and watch them pack the last oranges of the season?

We promise that we will, and the Bedouin bids us good-bye, jumps on to his "one-legged" horse, and disappears in the darkness.

ZOOLOGY

As great as my love is for Eretz Yisroel even so great is my aversion to snakes. When Dr. Mosensohn, about five years ago, came on a visit to America, I seized the first opportunity to ask him what the conditions were in Eretz Yisroel as to snakes.

His report was as follows:

"In Eretz Yisroel there are exactly one hundred different species of snakes. Ninety-eight of them are not dangerous. There's nothing to be afraid of as far as they are concerned. The remaining two, however, are really poisonous, only...."

"Only what?"

"Only Ahroni says that no man born of woman has ever seen those two species in Eretz Yisroel."

"And who is Ahroni?"

Ahroni is the zoologist of Eretz Yisroel who discovers all sorts of native animals and birds, and, in addition, discovers for every one of them a Hebrew name, which is an even more difficult task than discovering the animal or bird itself.

Coming to Rehoboth I learn that this self-same Ahroni lives but a stone's throw from our hotel, and I feel it my duty to pay him a call and thank him personally for the two species of poisonous snakes which, as he assures us, are not to be seen in Eretz Yisroel.

I climb the little hill opposite our hotel; I stride through the market-place, where a couple of Arabs are squatting on the ground, offering, for sale to the citizens of Rehoboth, oranges stolen from Rehoboth groves; I pass by the mail-shack and the eucalypti; then cross a wide street scarred by ruts, and stop before a tiny house.

From behind a high fence a big fowl sticks out a long neck at me, and stares at me out of round, glassy eyes. Evidently he has taken a strong dislike to me, for before I have had time to look him over, he struts angrily back to a corner of the enclosure, and refuses to grant me even a glance.

"Shalom"! The voice sounds like a trumpet, and reverberates across the opposite hill and throughout the quiet colony.

I turn and see before me the owner of the voice— a tall young man with a pale, freckled face, a long nose, fiery-red hair and a fiery-red moustache suggesting a cigar-lighter. He is dressed in white, his coat collar buttoned up to his neck, like a member of a sanitary corps or a hospital doctor. He offers me a warm, freckled hand, and casts a glance now at me and now at the queer fowl for whom he has in his other hand a little basket of chopped cactus-leaves.

I marvel at the fact that the cacti are without needles.

"That's my own discovery", he laughs, and his resounding tenor voice rolls off as far as the Mountains of Judea. "Your Luther Burbank of California worked for years and years in the attempt to develop cacti without spines, and to this day he has not fully succeeded. And here I've done the trick in a couple of minutes. All I used was my wife's cleaver."

He speaks now Hebrew, now German, and every other moment is swearing in Arabic. He refuses to pollute his lips with Yiddish. The Yiddishists—may their names and all memory of them be blotted out!

"Wallahi'l-'Azim! (by Allah the all-powerful), it is already two days since the creature hasn't taken a bite into his mouth. He runs about for days at a time like one possessed, and lives on fasting. He longs for the dry sands of the desert. It's too green and too beautiful here for him. You just wait and see. He won't touch even this succulent dish." And as he spoke the tall Ahroni opened a tiny door in the enclosure, bent down, cramping himself like a contortionist, and crept inside with the little basket of cacti in his hands. The ostrich looked at him through its cold, glassy eyes, and did not display the slightest appetite. He did display, however, a great desire to kick his owner in the stomach. Ahroni, it seems, was well acquainted with his ward's tricks, and beat a hasty retreat through the little door.

He tells me that for years he had pondered upon the plan of raising ostriches in Rehoboth, and of importing for that purpose a pair, not from Africa, but from the Syrian desert. So he went off and after great efforts and trouble procured what he wished. The transportation of the ostriches from the desert to Rehoboth was a task of stupendous proportions. For the specimen that I see here they first built a cage of thick stakes, but with his powerful legs he broke them to splinters and made a dash for freedom.

The door of the house is wide open and leads us into an obscure corridor, which serves also as the kitchen. From here we proceed to one of the two rooms which the father of Hebrew zoology occupies. This room serves the three-fold purpose of dining-room, study or library, and—museum. All of this refers only to daily uses, for by night the room is transformed into a bed-chamber for part of the specialist's family.

The walls are hung with frames into which are pinned hundreds of specimens representing every species of colored butterfly—every winged denizen of Eretz Yisroel that Ahroni had caught for years.

On the mantle-piece, on the window-sills, and on the book-shelves stood jars containing various species of preserved snakes, mice, lizards, and other equally attractive creatures, delightful to the eye of the zo-ologist. In the corner, underneath the frayed sofa, and wherever there was an inch of space, stood little boxes of eggs, stuffed birds, and every sort of rare creature. Ahroni began to name a few of them rapidly in Latin, German, and Hebrew. There are a good many Heb-rew names in the Mishnah, but many more must be invented. This requires a fundamental knowledge of Hebrew, a fine instinct for the spirit of the language, and an intimate acquaintance with the characteristic peculiarities of the specimens. To create a Hebrew terminology is the most difficult part of the task. He is now at work upon a zoological text-book intended specially for the students of Eretz Yisroel. He is already through with the animals and birds. Now he is working upon the fishes.

He tells me about the *Shefifon*—a tiny poisonous reptile which he found upon the roads in the Syrian desert. This *Shefifon* has a habit of hiding in the sand and waiting for a rider to approach. Then it jumps up and bites the horse's leg. Hence the biblical description: Like a *Shefifon* on the road.

"The study of the fauna of Eretz Yisroel", he says, in his resonant voice, at the same time waving his arms like a wind-mill, "helps us toward a better understanding of the Bible, and rectifies a great many errors that our forefathers harbored in Goluth.

Take for example, the verse, *Harhivi Korhatekh ka-Nesher*. How was that translated for you? Most likely in the same way that it was for me and all the other children that went to Hebrew school: 'Make large thy baldness as the eagle.' But what will you say if an eagle really does have a fine head of hair? The real truth is that *Nesher* is not an eagle at all, but signifies the same thing as the Arabic word *nisr*, a vulture, a bird that has not a trace of hair upon its head or even upon its neck. What, you doubt it? Wallahi 'l 'Azim! I can cite thirty proofs. In the first place...."

I begged to be excused. I assured him that I wasn't very exacting. From that day on, *nesher* to me would no longer mean eagle, even if all the kings of the east and the west should maintain the contrary.

He told me of the expedition in which he took part. That was years ago. Abdul Hamid was sultan at the time. With all his diplomatic cunning and blood-thirsty cruelty the sultan was a great lover of natural sciences. So he commissioned Professor Blankenhorn of Berlin to make an expedition through Turkey for the purpose of exploring the flora and fauna of his realm. Professor Blankenhorn invited Ahroni to become a member of the royal expedition. When Ahroni return-ed from the expedition he was offered the post of cur-ator of the sultan's zoological collection, at a very high salary, but he refused. His place was in Eretz Yisroel, and his labors belonged to the Jewish people. He wanted Hebrew learning and Eretz Yisroel zoologists to play a leading rôle in the world of zoological science. He showed me a pamphlet in which are described several new species just recently discovered. One of them is the "Bubo Bubo Ahroni", officially catalogued as first discovered by the zoologist "Ahroni of Rehoboth".

He smiled with pride, and his fiery moustache waxed even more fiery. He spoke with passionate heat, put-ting his heart and soul into every word, and his full tenor voice filled the small room, and the desiccated specimens fairly trembled in their frames on the walls.

En passant, I learned that he was a cousin of the world-famous tenor Yadlovker. The resonant voice is in the family.

A tall woman entered, with hair even redder than his. He introduces his wife. I can tell from her speech that she had plunged heart and soul into her hus-band's labors.

Ahroni looked at her and his eyes glistened with pride and love: "My wife has a better head than I. If she were to study zoology, she'd make a better zoologist than I."

She told me that they were studying English together. They get up at dawn. By day neither of them has any time. He is busy with his birds, and she has the house and the children to look after. She asked me to listen to her English, and I complied, discovering that for the short time they had been studying they have made astonishing progress.

"Without English", she explained to me, "Ahroni can do nothing." He was in London for the purpose of selling egg specimens to Rothschild, and his ignorance of English was a very great drawback. Whereupon they both resolved to learn English. In truth, only he needed to know it, but it's more agreeable when two study together. So both of them are studying it.

I am not an expert in zoology, but I was sufficiently a judge of English to see that she had done better at it than he.

A little fellow of about six appears in the doorway, and squeaks in a shrill voice: "Adon Ahroni, here's a big fly."

Whereupon Ahroni takes the big fly out of the tot's fingers, looks it over from every side, smacks his lips, and shakes his head with intense enthusiasm. Then he strokes the little fellow's hair, and says in his resonant tenor: "Todah (thanks), sonnie; it's trully a fine fly."

The child turns red to the ears, and jumps merrily out into the street to tell his companions what "Adon Ahroni" has said about his fly.

As soon as the child has gone, Ahroni lets the insect fly off through the window: "The children of the district bring me everything they find in the fields. Naturally, in ninety-nine cases out of a hundred they are of no account, but their intentions are good. They want to help me in my work."

Tea is suggested. Whereupon the zoological table must be cleared. First the books, small and large, then heaps of manuscripts, and last but not least, a little box of dried specimens. After the oil cloth had been cleared and cleaned, we sat down around the table. The zoologist and his wife upon the frazzled sofa, and I upon a chair that groaned at my every move.

I asked him whether it ever happened that one of his zoological specimens spoiled through lack of proper accommodations. The freckled face which up to now was aglow with cheerfulness became clouded. The red head bowed down; he looked at the jars and sighed: "It happened, it happened. In order to keep them as they really ought to be kept, a museum is needed. If I only had about four or five thousand francs I'd build a museum."

"What will you be able to do with such a small amount? The construction alone would cost more than that."

His wife intervenes: "Ahroni can't count beyond five

thousand francs. His competence in financial matters does not go any farther than that."

I am inquisitive to learn whether any of the Zionist leaders or institutions have ever displayed any interest in his work.

"There was some talk about giving a stipend of a thousand francs per year, but nothing came of it."

He became even gloomier, and it seemed that his voice was not quite so resonant as before: "You have unwittingly touched another, deeper wound. Just listen. I succeeded in obtaining, in the vicinity of Mount Lebanon, a young hart that had been shot. I believe it is the last of its kind, and the only specimen in the world. I have the hide and the skeleten ready to be stuffed. Any museum would be glad to acquire such a rarity. One foreign museum has offered me a very large price. But I'd rather sell the blown eggs of wild birds, and get along as best I could, than let out of Eretz Yisroel the last hart of its kind. I'll keep it for our first zoological museum, and we simply must have such a museum".

"Wallahi 'l'Azim! we'll have it. Only it's too bad that none of our leading public men gives himself any concern about the matter. Just imagine"—and in his excitement he sprang up—"a single specimen in the entire world, and in a people of thirteen million there's not a person to buy it for Eretz Yisroel."

His wife, who, in addition to studying English with the zoologist, was compelled to resort to the utmost economy in household affairs—"to split a groat in two"—sat with her hands folded in her lap, listening to her husband as big tears rolled down her cheeks.

In the self-same room where we sat around to tea, deciding that the Jewish people deserved to be hanged, I happened, several weeks later, to be present at one of the most beautiful and joyous scenes that I have ever beheld.

It was a holiday, and the children from the schools of the surrounding colonies had come together with their teachers to inspect "Adon Ahroni's museum." Since the room was very small, and the number of pupils quite large, the pupils were let in ten or fifteen at a time, and as soon as one small group went out, another entered.

In the middle of the room, near the table, stood the red-headed Ahroni, and his face was beaming. Stuffed animals and birds, brought to light from under the sofa and from the boxes that stood in the corner, were heaped upon the table. The children, with eyes aglow and flaming cheeks, pressed around the tall zoologist on all sides, the smaller ones in front, the older ones behind.

"Children! Do you see this bird? He has a very long beak, and lives on the fish that he catches under water...."

Every one of the children had to touch the bird with his own fingers—if not feel it all over, at least touch the tip of the beak or a feather. And Ahroni saw to it that nobody was slighted. All sort of childish questions filled the air. Ahroni answered in his usual, vibrant voice, describing how the birds feed, how they sleep, how they build nests, and how they protect themselves against their enemies. As he spoke he introduced all manner of funny anecdotes and the children nearly burst with laughter. The teachers who had come with the children were infected with the laughter, and so were the insects and the specimens on the walls, and so were the lizards in the jars.

COMING AND GOING

We are no longer the sole guests at our hotel. Each day brings new arrivals, diverse types of Jews from various countries. Among the new comers are long-bearded, pious Jews who, when a hair comes out of their beards, place it between the leaves of the Zohar. And then there are such as have not the slightest sign of Jewishness upon their faces or in their speech, and one has to take their word for it.

Yesterday three new guests arrived. They were all respectable Hasidim from the vicinity of Kalish. One, with a thick brown beard, is the overseer of a large estate. And he bears proofs of this. The thumb of his right hand is missing. He was showing the farm-hands how to work a threshing-machine, whereupon the threshing-machine became too hasty and removed his thumb. These three Jews have come here to see whether they cannot purchase, at a reasonable price, a tract of land or a Biyare. If they can find the right thing, they will go back home, liquidate their business, and bring their families here.

The overseer, from the very first moment, became intimate with me. At the beginning he discussed some biblical verses. He expatiated on the passage "and the children of Israel went out with a high hand" (Exodus 14.8). And as he did so, he wiggled the stump where his thumb would have been were it not for the threshing-machine.

Little by little he poured out his heart to me. Had we met in Kalish, it is likely that he would never have engaged in so deep a discussion with a beardless fellow like me. But he knows that I have come to Eretz Yisroel from a great distance, and that we have both been driven thither by the same yearning. So he spoke to me as if I were an old friend.

He has become tired of living in Goluth. He does not lack the best of everything. No matter how well things may go with him in Eretz Yisroel, he will never enjoy there such plenty as he enjoys in his present home. But he is not in quest of fortune. Bread to eat and a garment to wear for himself and his family— that is all he desires.

The youngest of the group, a fellow of about forty-five, is enchanted with everything. He can't remain for a moment in any place. Every instant he runs out of the hotel, drinks in a draught of sunshine, takes a look at the houses, the trees, at the sky, and returns all smiles and happiness. He arose early at dawn and left at once, with a great velvet prayer-bag under his arm, for the synagogue. He did not return till eleven o'clock, when the table was already set for the noonday meal. His face was radiant. He was in no hurry for breakfast. Evidently it was not even in his thoughts. He kept on rubbing his palms together and saying in a half sing-song tone:

"What a precious land! What a dear land!"

"THE LAND OF THE SHALOMS"

At our hotel there's a German Zionist, the engineer T. He is a husky fellow, of medium build, in his forties. He dresses only in khaki. On his head he wears an English pith helmet, and on his feet high boots. Most of the time he travels to the hotel on a tiny donkey. T. was bred and born in Germany, but he has seen a great deal of the world. He was for a long time in South America, then in the Unted States. Later he accepted a position under the German government as an engineer in one of the German colonies of South Africa. From South Africa he wandered to Eretz Yisroel, but after a short time his *wanderlust* drove him back to Africa. This is the second time that he has been in Palestine. He tells me that the first time he came from Africa he brought along as his servant a semi-savage, a black Kaffir. When the Kaffir returned to Africa, he used to call Eretz Yisroel the Land of the Shaloms.

T. has come to Rehoboth to take care of the work on the road that is being laid between Rehoboth, Rishon l'Zion, and Jaffa. There is a tale about this road, the essence of which is as follows: For years and years the Jewish colonists of Rehoboth and Rishon l'Zion had been seeking from the Turkish government permission to lay a road at their own expense, but it had been utterly impossible for them to receive governmental consent.

One official passed them on to the other, and everywhere palms were stretched out for Bakshish. Only after it had cost the colonists something like fifty thousand francs in bribes, and after a procrastination of years, did the permission arrive, containing, however, the rather inconsistent stipulation—that the road be begun at once, and that it be completed not later than a year from date.

The building of the road has only just begun. In the meantime, if one wishes to go from Rehoboth to Jaffa one must reserve a place in the *diligence* a day ahead. On the following day the passenger must get up very early, for at half-past six the packed coach is already on its way. The journey to Jaffa takes about four hours by the clock, although one is actually riding only one hour. The balance of the time you trudge up to the ankles in sand together with eight or nine other persons. And in the meantime Mahmud works with might and main to get the horses to pull the empty coach. As the passengers trudge through the sand, they get into conversation, and discuss everything under the sun.

Once, as we were thus trudging along — a whole company of Jews—escorting the empty coach with great ceremony, one of our travelling companions, a colonist from Rehoboth, gave us a whole chapter of the history connected with the early years of the settlement.

It was against the law at that time to build a new structure without the permission of the government, and to get the required permit took more money than the building itself cost. Because of this, it was often necessary for entire families to live under the open sky. Whenever they wanted to put up a house or a barn they'd have to hurry day and night so as to fininsh before a *hayyal* (soldier) would show up. Once the building was up to the roof, there was no more fear. They would not be told to pull it down.

It happened once in the very midst of the construction that a *hayyal* put in an appearance. What was to be done? The ragged, hungry gendarme interfered and refused to let the work go on. There was no time to be lost. Whereupon no time was wasted in discussion, and the fellow was seized bodily, bound hand and foot and thrown into a room, while the construction was rushed for all it was worth.

A day went by and the *hayyal* commenced to feel the gnawings of hunger, so he began to sue for peace. The colonists gave him his choice: either to starve upon the altar of duty, which death has no very strong appeal to a Turkish official, or help in the construction of the house and get a *bishlik* per day. After some haggling, they agreed upon a *bishlik* and a half per day, and the *hayyal* proved to be an excellent worker.

Together with us there trudged and panted an elderly Jew who has come to Eretz Yisroel for a few months. He cannot praise Eretz Yisroel sufficiently. His wife, however, a tall stout woman, interrupts him, and unburdens herself of her plaints and tribulations.

"In the first place," she says, "there is no horse-radish here. Where did anybody ever hear of such a thing—horse-radish must be imported from Russia!"

Somebody consoles her with the observation that since there is no fish to be had here either, the lack of horse-radish makes little difference.

"Well, as far as the horse-radish is concerned, I could do without it," continued the woman. "But the coins! It's enough to turn one crazy. At the hotel in Jaffa we paid in francs. The Arab who brought us here on his donkey, we had to pay in *bishliks*, and when you come to the train, more money trouble. Transactions there are reckoned in *mejediehs*. But this is only the beginning. This morning I bought a packet of note paper, and the dealer asked three *tholer*. I could no longer restrain myself. 'You ought to be ashamed of yourself', I say to him. 'To be sure, this is Eretz Yisroel, but how can a person have the gall to ask three *tholers* for twenty sheets of paper'. The Jewish dealer looks at me, and his sides shake with laughter. It appears that a *tholer* is a *grush* and a *grush* is three *metallik*, and that a *metallik* amounts in all to two kopeks."

A young woman from Rehoboth, with clever, black eyes, adds fuel to the flame. She tells her that the value of a *metallik* is not the same in all cities, and that even in the self-same city the value is not always the same.

At this point a young fellow near me joins the talk, and relates that an acquaintance of his had occasion to change a twenty-franc piece into other coins, and these other coins into a still different coinage, and when he was through with the exchange he had two and a half francs left. The remainder had disappeared in the different processes of exchange.

The fellow is evidently a wag, but his account stirs the discontented one to a fresh outburst.

"Moreover", she turns to me, "where in all the world has anybody ever seen people without any 'Good mornings', or 'Good evenings', or 'How do you do's'? And no 'Good health to you', but always the same old 'shalom' here and 'shalom' there. I'm so weary of it that, believe me, if anybody accosted me with a good old-fashioned 'How do you do', I'd fall upon his neck and kiss him right in public."

In the meantime the *diligence* drives in amidst the vineyards of Rishon l'Zion. On both sides of the road are hedges of wild cactus—huge, unsightly distortions twisted one into the other, and everywhere bristling with sharp needles. Because of their spiny quality, they make excellent fences.

I tell the woman a story. Once upon a time a great number of people came to settle here. The land was rich and fertile, the air was a delight, and the sun was ready to bring forth the sweetest fruits from the trees and the very best products of the earth. But the people didn't care to till the land, or dig it; every day they were seized with a new whim. They trumped up every sort of accusation against the land. So the land became a desert, and its inhabitants scattered to the four corners of the earth. And a decree went forth from heaven that as soon as one of the deserters should die, he should be transformed into a cactus bush and have to guard the fields against which he had uttered evil words.

And there they stand now—the sinful souls—in the form of ugly, spiny cacti, guarding the heavily-laden vines that were planted by industrious hands, listening to the merry songs of those who fill their baskets with red, luscious grapes.

POOR RELATIONS

One of the chums of the Yemenite maid who works for the A.'s is being married to-night. So the servant has invited her mistress to attend the ceremony. It is decided that we shall all go together.

The night spreads its black cloak over the colony. We go through a dark by-path. On one side a thick hedge of mimosa, and on the other a *pardes* of olive-trees. The sweet fragrance of the mimosa and the dewy gardens breathe cool air into our faces. The stars in the sky grow momentarily more numerous and larger. About us there is the quietude of a burial-ground. One can hear the dew-drops fall from leaf to leaf.

Madame A. leads the way, and we follow. She is a native of the colony, and could find her way blindfolded. All at once we turn into a narrow lane. To the right, a large garden, to the left tiny cottages whitening in the darkness. Amidst the cottages there are saplings and garden-patches. Not a glimmer of light anywhere.

After we have advanced a hundred paces we hear a commotion and a racket, and catch sight of a light shining from one of the cottages falling upon a banana-bush opposite to it.

We enter a small yard, and find ourselves in the midst of a gathering of little girls about twelve or thirteen years of age. They are seated in a semi-circle singing a monotonous, tearfully gloomy tune.

Where have I heard that tune before? And from a

dark recess of my memory the resemblance darts forth. Thus sang the daughters of Gilead, bemoaning Jephthah's daughter. Somewhere above hangs a tiny lantern, and the yellow, flickering flame heightens the darkness. In a corner sits one of the girls, beating time with her hands upon a sort of tambourine. The sad moaning in the darkness does not cease for a moment. The small girls, as it appears later, are young wives. This may be recognized from the black kerchiefs they wear across their foreheads. A few of them are mothers, who have already buried infants.

From among the tiny figures stands out that of a strong, tall young wife of twenty. I recognized her. It is Miriam, the maidservant of Khawaja Musa. Her husband is a Yemenite from Petach Tikvah. She ran away from him because he used to beat her so mercilessly. One day he appeared with all his relatives, armed with sticks and a rope, ready to fetter his wife and take her back with him by force. Miriam, who is ordinarily a heroic woman, as soon as she caught sight of her husband, began to tremble like a leaf. She nearly died of fright. Luckily, Khawaja Musa was at home. He gave her husband more than he was looking for, and chased him away from the house.

Miriam's only brother was at first very much ashamed of her conduct. Her husband has paid for her, like an honest man, so she belonged to him. To oppose him was a horrible sin. But the brother came around to her point of view. As guardian of his sister he gets everything she earns. So that he loses nothing after all by his sister's recalcitrance.

Madame A. points out the bride to me—a puny, weak girl of about eleven or twelve, with a beautiful, dark face and deep, black eyes—the joint heirloom of Jews and Arabs. The little bride is attired in a green dress with red flowers, and in a white veil. On her head is a sort of silver diadem, and around her neck a string of coral beads and silver coins. Heavy silver ear-rings are weighting down her tiny dark ears, and on both wrists she wears silver bracelets. Her fingers are stained with henna and covered with rings. Our cicerone explains to us that the jewelry does not belong to the bride. How does she come by such a treasure? It is borrowed from every relative who owns anything, and from acquaintances and neighbors, so as to beautify the bride on the wedding-day.

The sad chorus wails and moans, and the tambourine beats a mournful accompaniment. In the middle of the circle two women are whirling around. They are dancing a fantastic kosher-dance. One of them looks like an aged woman. Her face is wrinkled and withered, her bosom flat, her figure lean.

Madame A. knows all the Yemenites of Rehoboth, and tells me that the aged woman is not yet forty.

"For that matter, they'll never tell anybody their age. They fear the evil eye."

"And this is one of Shalom's wives!"

I turn around. A charming little maid of about fourteen holds her head at a graceful slant, rocks to and fro, chiming in with the mournful chorus.

"Who is Shalom?"

"Shalom is a celebrity. You must know Shalom. He has an entire harem. The business pays him. A Yemenite woman doesn't cost much. You can buy one for about two hundred francs. That is much cheaper than among the Arabs. The lowest price among them is five hundred francs. So that there are many old bachelors. Take, for example, my father's Arabagi (driver); it's really a pity. He's a chap nearing his forties, and can't save up enough to buy a wife."

"But what about Shalom?"

"Shalom has four wives, three of them in Rehoboth and the other in Jaffa. They all earn money. They are servants. Besides the fact that they all hand him everything they earn, the Rehoboth wives, when they come home in the evening, bring him the suppers that their mistresses give them. The one you see here is his fourth. When he married her she was eight and he— a man of more than thirty"

We go in among the men. A tiny cave-like house consisting of one floorless room. A small lamp flickers. The crowd is seated upon the ground, around the walls. There is no trace of furniture. They drink black coffee from diminutive cups, and smoke narghilehs. There are no windows, and the smoke hangs like a dense cloud over the red fezes and the woven turbans. Some of the guests wear shoes—in honor of the wedding. The others are barefoot.

At the head sits the groom, a youth of about eighteen, wearing a prayer-shawl. In his hand he holds a large bouquet of wild flowers. As a new guest enters, he approaches the groom, whereupon the latter arises, and both place their hands upon their hearts, then upon their foreheads, and kiss each other several times upon both cheeks. Women enter—evidently close relatives of the groom—and kiss his hand.

Not far from the groom sits a powerful fellow of about thirty, with a fine face adorned with a thick black beard, and with large, dirty bare feet. Before him he holds an old manuscript, and sings a chant in a mixture of Hebrew and Arabic. As he sings, he accompanies himself with an iron rod upon a sort of a copper tray. His voice is shrill and metallic. When he finishes a verse, the echo of his voice resounds like that of a bell just rung. The tune is half gleeful, half doleful.

Before the groom three young men weave themselves into a sort of fantastic reel. One places his hands upon the shoulders of the next. The movements are very graceful and filled with the mute sorcery of dark Eastern nights.

We convey our congratulations and our "Mazzal Tov" to the groom. We receive the reply "Mazzal Uberakhah" (good luck and blessing).

Low stools are brought in our honor.

"Bevakkashah."

We are offered home-made wine, black honey-cakes, and baked corn. We taste the wine and our teeth are set on edge. Pungent and sour. As to the cake, I am afraid to risk a trial. In front of us stand a couple of little bright-eyed urchins with begrimed faces, looking yearningly at the royal treat that we have been offered and licking their chops like hungry kittens. I take the cake and give to it them. They seize it and dash out.

We have come too late. The ceremony took place an hour before. Now they will sing and dance until late into the night. Then will come the supper, served to the men in one room and to the women in another.

At supper there will be meat and thick soup. The meat together with the soup will be served in a single bowl, and they'll eat as the children of Israel ate the paschal lamb, not letting the food cool and devouring it in a hurry; nor will God's gift be defiled by a fork. The soup will be sopped up with soft "pittes", and you may be sure that not a drop will go to waste.

A SECOND VISIT

I have been once again to the Yemenites. This time it was in the bright sunshine of a Friday afternoon. Like Eliezer, the servant of Abraham, I stopped where the Yemenite housewives come to get their water. On account of the approaching Sabbath women were constantly arriving—old and young—with the vessels upon their heads. Had those vessels been pitchers, I should have compared them with Rebekah. But for the most part they were Nobel's kerosene cans.

These cans, as well as the wooden crates in which they are shipped from Baku or America, serve in Eretz Yisroel a hundred different purposes of which the kerosene seller could never have dreamed. I have even seen a coffin for a child made out of a kerosene box.

The women looked aged and ugly. But their gait was erect and proud, and the tango-girls of New York might well have come to them to learn the art of walking beautifully and with grace. This erect, royal bearing the Yemenite and the Arab women owe to their custom of carrying burdens upon their heads. The head thus learns to hold itself erect, and the limbs to maintain a symmetrical balance.

My companion began to make preparations for photographing the group. Some of them ran off helter-skelter, others hesitated, and the braver ones remained. All they asked was a picture.

A group of elderly Yemenites returned from their labor with their picks on their shoulders. No sooner had they caught sight of the camera than they quickly withdrew. Four young Yemenite laborers stopped. I turn to one of them whose ear-locks reach *only* to his ear-lobes. It appears that he belongs to the "new" faction—to the Pirhe Teman (Flowers of Yemen), and knows of Bialik's poetry. I get into conversation with him, and begin by asking him how it is that the Yemenites take unto themselves so many wives.

"Here", he answers, blushing, "we ordinarily take only one. Yonder, in Yemen, they used to take more. But that was solely for the sake of children. The children die one after another, and a single wife isn't enough for the perpetuation of the race."

"And how about Shalom?"

"Shalom", interposes another, "is a cloven-footed animal. He blackens our reputation in the eyes of the Ashkenazim. That's why the Ashkenazim can feel so proud and look down upon the Temonim."

They are eager to make a good showing before the Ashkenazim, so that the latter may not treat them with benevolent condescension.

I was recently told by Z. that when he built his luxurious villa, a Yemenite hod-carrier boasted that in Yemen, even the poorest of them, dwelt in a far more beautiful house.

We pass a blind old Temoni sunning himself, and we come to the shack of the old teacher. He is seated before the door, his feet coiled under him, surrounded by a group of tiny pupils—a ragged, tattered crew, with black, fiery little eyes. In his right hand is a long rod, which has evidently been working hard all week. As it was just before the call to the synagogue, the old teacher had prepared to give each of his pupil's a final lash, which was to serve as a signal that school was over, and also a reminder that there were rods in the world.

When the kodak was pointed at him, he turned his face away and began to shout: "What do you want of me? Go your way. I know what you want that for."

"What for?"

"You'll exhibit the picture in foreign lands and collect alms by aid of it, and you won't give us a thing".

Yet, by a trick, we managed to snap him and his school.

The Temonim have grudges and complaints a-plenty against the Ashkenazim. In the first place, they took with them into exile the golden table of the Temple, and that's why they're so rich. They, the Yemenites, were always treated unfairly. Ezra the Scribe did not even take them with him into Eretz Yisroel. And for that God punished him and he lies buried in Babylon. It was not given to him to die on sacred soil. The name of Ezra is boycotted by them to this very day. No Yemenite is named Ezra.

They have no love for the Ashkenazim, but they are silent in their presence. Now and then a harsh word escapes.

Not long ago, at a meeting of Yemenites, the "new" and the "old" factions got into a quarrel, and one of them sprang up and shouted at the other: "Ashkenazi!"

On the way back I meet an old Temoni who is dressed in his Sabbath clothes—a faded black frock coat of a fashionable European cut which, in a previous existence, graced the back of some Rehoboth dandy. I get into conversation with him, and gradually we approach the subject of spirits.

"They say that there are many spirits in Yemen".

"There certainly are," he nods. "There are Yemenites who have slain armies of them. There are all sorts. There are some spirits that look just like human beings and act just like them".

"There is David, who lived among these spirits for two years and barely escaped with his life."

"Where is David?"

"David is in Rehoboth, and lives not far from here."

Before I have a chance to ask another question, he begins to tell, in his Yemenite Hebrew, the whole story about David and the spirits. Every Yemenite knows this story as he knows his own name.

David was a highly respected member of the community. The spirits cast an eye upon him. In fact, their intention was to make him one of their own. And there was a certain elderly spirit who was after him more than any. Now the *parnas* of the spirits is held by them in great reverence. He had a daughter —a striking beauty—and he took it into his head to have David for a son-in-law. And when the *shedim* determine on anything, then God help us.

So once, while David was bathing in the stream, they lay in ambush for him, seized him and spirited him away beyond all the seven seas, where they have a vast realm. David struggled, wept, and entreated. But it was of no avail. The prospective father-in-law insists, and there stands the bride as radiant as the full moon. And the *hakham* of the spirits, an old man with a handsome countenance, has come to officiate at the ceremony. So they brought forth the wedding canopy, had a wonderful seven days' feast, and David became the husband of a female spirit.

He was not permitted to go out of the house. They gave him the best of food and drink. He could have all that his heart desired. But his spirit wife did not let him out of her sight. She kept hugging him and kissing him and daily revealing greater love for him.

Thus passed two full years, during which his beautiful spirit wife bore David two children.

But David didn't care for such a life. For days and days he went about like a madman, and by night he could not close his eyes. How could he get rid of her? Whereupon the Lord, blessed be His name, sent him the inspiration to go before the old *hakham* of the spirits and open his bitter heart to him.

So David managed to have his spirit spouse release him for a couple of hours. He swore that he would not run away. Off he went to the *hakham*, and so soon as he reached him, he fell upon his knees and began to wail: "Rabbi, have pity. How long must I suffer?"

The old man's heart was touched. He was of a very compassionate nature. So he said to David: "Go home, *habibi*, I will do my best for you."

And the *hakham* at once called a meeting, and laid the affair before the assembly. Whereupon there ensued a tumult and confusion, and terrible dissension arose among the spirits. One faction was in favor of having David released, but the side representing David's father-in-law asserted that he must remain with his wife and children. But the *hakham* of the spirits ruled that David must be allowed to go home, and whatever the *hakham* says is sacred. The spirits made but a single condition: that before he be released, each of them might pluck out one of his hair.

When David awoke next morning, he found himself in his own house in Yemen, with his wife and offspring. And when he told them where he had been all that time, what had happened to him, and how he came to be rescued, they all offered up the prayer: "Blessed be He who bringeth back the dead to life."

But when he began to put on his phylacteries in preparation for prayers, he discovered that he hadn't a hair on his head. It was a great shame for him to have to go about without ear-locks, so his wife cut off a few tresses from their eldest little girl, and glued them to his temples instead of ear-locks.

The hair never grew back, and David wears the pasted ear-locks to this very day.

SUN-STRANDS

Quite unexpectedly our hotel has received a large number of guests. The Yiddish novelist Ash and his wife have arrived from Galilee. They intend to stay here for a while.

Together with Ash came a Petrograd millionaire, and old Feinberg, with snow-white hair, the distributor of "Aunt" ICA'S alms in Russia.

Ash's room is right opposite mine. Between us lies the long dining-room. So we keep visiting each other.

There's a knock at the door.

"Yavo!"

In comes Ash. I receive him with great ceremony, invite him to sit down upon the only chair at hand, and treat him to *bon-bons*, which are wrapped in papers bearing Herzl's picture.

It is decided that he has been visiting long enough, and that I must repay the call. So Ash goes back to his room, and before he has closed his door behind him, I knock at it.

"Yavo!"

He receives me with great pomp, and offers me white tartelettes. And thus passes an entire bright day.

We often go strolling through the avenue of mimosa and eucalyptus-trees, and from that point we take a long walk as far as Khawaja Musa's orchard. The whole landscape is spread about us in a single sheet of sunshine, and the road over which we pass is thickly planted on both sides with wild flowers of every color.

We speak of everything under the sun, and above all, of Yiddish literature. And the bright sun around us draws forth from us hidden hopes and plans that would never have the courage to reveal themselves amidst ordinary surroundings. All dreams here become endowed with the strength of Samson.

We have a complete plan for issuing all the Yiddish classics in the best style, and in a uniform edition, which will aid to spread the knowledge of Yiddish literature and will be the pride and joy of all friends of the Yiddish tongue.

Money? Maecenases will be found to further the plan. Moreover, the publishers will lose nothing by the job. The edition will prove a huge success, and the books will sell like hot cakes.

In addition to the plan for an edition of the Yiddish classics, which is intented for the *goluth*, we have a more romantic plan for Eretz Yisroel.

We will purchase near Rehoboth a large tract of land and found a colony to consist solely of the elite: writers, authors, poets, great composers, painters, sculptors.

Already we can see just how this colony and its beautiful villas will appear. Every house will be a dream in brick and mortar. Before each house, a garden of the most beautiful flowers and plants. The streets will be broad, bordered on each side with grass plots. Everything will be a joy to the eye and an aesthetic delight to poet and artist. We begin to make a list of those whom we shall invite to the colony. There will be no lack of applicants. There will be too many, in fact. What great Jewish artist will not be eager to build himself a villa in our *colonie d'élite*? Mischa Elman, Zimbalist, Schnitzler—not to mention the nationalistic Yiddish writers.

When we broached our plan to the colonist G., his imagination beheld even brighter visions than ours. A wonderful plan. Not far from the colony was just the tract of land we wanted. It belonged to a former colonist who was at that time in New York. He would write to him at once. He thought that he would get the land at a very reasonable price. So the land problem is settled.

There is in Rehoboth a young, undersized, blond agriculturist of about thirty. His father is a Russian Jew who settled in Belgium and became there a wealthy diamond merchant. The son studied agriculture and went off to Brazil, where he occupied a professorship in an agricultural school. He came thence to this place, to act as overseer of the large orange-grove that his father and several other Belgian Jews had bought in Rehoboth. He makes the acquaintance of both Ash and myself, and invites us to visit him.

He is still a bachelor, but lives in a beautiful house with all the European comforts possible in Rehoboth. He shows us his books, his pictures, and antiques. We are in no hurry with our admiration, however. We wait until he offers us his choice liqueurs, and only then do we praise his fine taste with a truly easy conscience.

At last—

He extracts from a drawer an elegantly bound volume, and begins to read me his French verses. He is an excellent declaimer. The French nasal sounds impart a solemn tone to his reading. I see that he is highly exalted by his recitation. My eyes seek Ash's in quest of aid. Why only me? And I notice that Ash has finished his Benedictine, and sneaked into the next room, leaving me to my fate.

Nor is this the only time that I was thus abandoned. Once, as we were walking along through the colony, a young workman approached us, dressed in Bedouin garments, and before we knew anything at all, he drew forth from his bosom—a poem. He is a shomer in a vineyard. He lives "close to nature", and is on the most intimate terms with starry nights. And he wants expert opinion upon his work.

Ash swears that he is no expert, so the fellow turns to me. I can't offer the same excuse. I want to be original. So I tell him to come some other time.

Now Ash was only visiting Rehoboth, and soon left. So that I had the Yiddishist Bedouin on my hands for a long time after.

The story of the hart that could find no Jewish purchaser had never left my mind since the day that Ahroni first told it to me. When the millionaire from Petrograd arrived at our hotel, it occurred to me that it would be an excellent idea to interest him in that animal. Perhaps he would be moved.

They tell me in Rehoboth that he is worth not a kopek less than fifteen million rubles. And perhaps more.

In Tel-Aviv they say that it isn't quite fifteen, but it's at least six. So I say to myself that he certainly has three millions, and since the rare hart specimen may be bought for a mere four or five hundred rubles, he surely will not say a word, but open his purse at once, saying: "Such a mere trifle!"

So, together with Ash, I took him to Ahroni's. The zoologist showed him bugs, bees, flies, mice, and birds. We looked on in continuous ecstasy. In the meantime, through a skilful cross-examination, I draw out from Ahroni the whole history of his zoological activities and also of the support that he doesn't get, together with the account of the difficulties under which he must pursue his labors and—the story of the hart. Let the millionaire know.

Ash gets excited, and heaps fire and brimstone upon the ingratitude of the Jewish people. And I keep vociferating that it is a blot on our conscience, looking at the millionaire out of a corner of my eye.

Listening to our talk, Madame Ahroni recalls their pitiful plight, and all at once bursts into bitter tears.

Long life to Madame Ahroni. Her tears could not have come more opportunely. This will help.

The millionaire doesn't say a word. But I know that he has been deeply stirred. His eyes, methinks, are somewhat moist. The rare hart is already ours. And unless I am greatly mistaken, Ahroni will have a house of his own and a yearly stipend.

But we do not desist. There is still a jar containing a tiny serpent. Let him see that, too. Let him see

Ahroni's greatness, and give with a lavish hand. The millionaire looked at the serpent, and his hand rose.

My heart leaped. His hand was going to his pocket.

How much? A thousand, perhaps, with a promise to give more later.

His hand rises, and rises, and comes to a pause opposite his—mouth.

The millionaire's face expands in a broad yawn, and he says: "It's late. Time to go to sleep."

THE HAGIGAH

Dear......

To my good fortune the septennial folk-feast was held after all, in Rehoboth, during the five intermediary days of Passover.

On account of the murder trial going on between the Arabs of the village of Zarnuka and the colonists of Rehoboth, it was at first considered most advisable not to rouse the neighbors by a great Jewish gathering. Moreover, Petach Tikvah, the largest of the Jewish colonies in Judea, had long envied Rehoboth its feast, and wished to make the holiday a function of its own. But it was decided that the custom should not be broken. The inhabitants of Rehoboth had a seven years' right to the celebration. So the feast was held in Rehoboth, and turned out to be more beautiful and festive than ever.

The preparations for the great occasion had begun weeks before. The members of the celebration committee were up to their ears in work. First, the *Mekom ha-Hagigah*—a large open place near the colony —had to be swept clean and roped off. Then booths had to be erected for the various exhibitions, a platform for the speakers, poles for climbing, and so on. In addition to this, a low-priced buffet had to be put up under the open sky, so that those who came from a distance should be able to purchase, at the price of a few *metalliks*, matzoth, eggs, cheese, and coffee, or tea.

Everybody worked at the preparations for the festival with the same industrious gusto and enthusiasm with which pious Jews roll the special matzoth for the Passover Seder nights. The nearer the feast day approached the more feverish and impatient the people became. They spoke of the feast of the previous year, and of two years ago, and three years past. They prayed for clear weather, and that nothing should interfere with the celebration, and figured in advance the number of prominent guests that would attend the function this year.

During the whole morning of the feast, and on the day before, all the roads that lead to the colony were dense with people. The young folk came on horseback, and their horses were decorated, in Bedouin fashion, with tassels and fringes. Others rode upon tiny asses that were far stronger than they looked. Here and there strode a camel, balancing on his hump Jewish maidens from a near-by settlement. Wagons, carts, coaches, and *diligences*, packed with passengers, as well as a large number of pedestrians, journeyed over the sandy tracts into the colony. The Jaffa-Jerusalem railroad company ran special trains between Jaffa and Ramleh. From there the passengers came to Rehoboth on donkeys.

There wasn't room for even a pin in our hotel. There were guests from every part of Europe, from America, from New Zealand. The whole colony buzzed like a bee-hive. The weather seemed to have been made to order for the festivities.

S., who came with the Zionist "Revision Committee",

was invited to deliver the festival oration. S. is not of a nervous temperament, nor is he a man of moods. He had written and spoken so much during his time on every conceivable occasion, that it was hard to imagine that he would be perturbed or excited, or get stage-fright before delivering a speech.

This time he certainly was excited and upset. It could be seen from his face. The solemnity of the day, the significance of the moment, deprived even him of his usual calm and self-confidence.

Now I have become a *Hajj*. This is the name given by the Muslims to one who has been to Mecca and beheld the holy Ka'bah. And I have been in Rehoboth and beheld the Hagigah. This is a title that I shall henceforth assume.

I was standing near the Beth-'Am (town hall). Around me seethed a thousand-headed multitude garbed in every sort of Oriental and semi-Oriental dress. They were preparing for the procession around the colony, with which the festival generally begins. From above, a blue sky looked down—an Eretz Yisroel sky—and the sun—an Eretz Yisroel sun—drenched every head with its rays. All at once the Rishon l'Zion band burst into a spirited march, and all hearts began to flutter. I knew that what was dancing and thrilling in me at the moment was dancing and thrilling in every one of the thousands that I could see all about me— the same sorrows were ours, and now the same joys.

A nation has risen from the dead. How has this happened? Who has accomplished it? Who has brought about this miracle? Who has been the Messiah here, and who the redeemer?

Next to me stood a merchant from Russia. A practical, shrewd business man who had been jesting and belittling everything and everybody all morning long. For everything he had a joke or a cynical word. Now he turned away from me lest I should catch sight of his tears.

Later I was standing on one of the hills from which the Mekom ha-Hagigah is approached, and gazed down upon the vast multitude. The majority wore white or straw hats, and when they moved about, it looked as if a light summer breeze had sprung up and was blowing through a field of white daisies.

S. took his place upon the speakers' platform, spoke in Hebrew, and began: "The father of Zionism said: 'If you so wish it, it is no longer a fairy-tale!' I say more: Whether you wish it or not, it is no longer a fairy-tale."

Behind the speaker, in the far distance, spread the green almond groves and the silver-gray olive orchards, and further still, the mountains of Judea, behind their thin veil of mist, rubbed their eyes.

When had they beheld such a holiday before?

When S. finished his speech, the Shomerim discharged their guns into the air, and Jewish horsemen exhibited all kinds of "fantasias" on their fleet-footed steeds.

There were exhibitions of various products of the new settlement. Poor, scant—but a firm purpose is evident in every direction.

I went over to the booths above which hung a sign "Perfumes made from Carmel and Sharon flowers." So I bought a phial, made in Austria or Germany and filled with the odors of Carmel and Sharon. It is worth pondering. Carmel and Sharon alone are not sufficient. In Eretz Yisroel the rôle of *goiuth* grows clearer and clearer to me, and so do the spiritual riches that we have willingly or unwillingly accumulated during our wandering—the purification and the cleansing that we have received. A glance at the low cultural state of the Arabs, to whom the sun has become a curse instead of a blessing, is enough to make the whole matter clear to me. Islam, born under the bluest of skies and in a sea of sunshine, is the gloomiest faith on earth.

...How much have the snows and the northern storms given us! Now we will transplant the treasures of the snows in the land of eternal verdure. We will transplant the gifts of storm and winter in the land of beauty and sunshine. And there will burgeon forth a wonder-blossom—a union of the Orient that gave the world a God, and the Occident that gave man to himself and taught him the enjoyment of his own strength.

However dear Eretz Yisroel may be to us, it is yet not sufficiently so for us to receive it in exchange for our share in the joint heritage of the nations. We will renounce nothing and not a single step backward will we take. Eretz Yisroel must be all gain to us.

...Once again we are pilgrims. But whither? Not to the cold walls of Jerusalem, but to living, fresh, growing life. We go on a pilgrimage to the golden oranges, to the vines.

Even the old people who come to Eretz Yisroel to worship the Lord, begin to understand that the God of Israel dwells amidst the vineyards and the almond-groves. We have here octogenarians and even nona-genarians who have settled in Rehoboth for the express purpose of spending day and night in study and prayer.

All of our previous holidays have been reminiscences of the past. This is the first holiday that is a welcome to the future.

. . . Now I can hear the buds bursting. I know that everywhere there is growth and multiplication. And my text is the old one: "It may be long in coming, but daily I await its arrival." It has already arrived. The under-soil is full of sap, and everything that we shall sow and plant will flourish. There will be an abundant yield.

The far, far future stretches out its arms, and entwines the old past, drawing it over to itself. Above us and within us, whether we are aware of it or not, this junction of past and future is always going on.

My heart overflows, and I am burdened with an immense wealth. I would like to pour it forth in a single, vast, glowing word. But it is not granted to me. I envy him who will sing the great song of Eretz Ysroel. Here upon the soil of Eretz Yisroel will that song be created.

That great and beautiful song is growing now, and the God-gifted one who shall come to chant it will pluck it as easily as I pluck a yellow daisy.

In the evening there was a concert in the "town hall". There were fireworks, too, and the settlement echoed with song. The two hotels could accommodate but a few. The hospitality of the colonists came to the rescue. But a large number were obliged to sleep under the open starry sky.

Two girls climbed up a broad tree, and spent the night there as best they could.

It's a glorious thing to be here. When you come to this beautiful land, you yourself will become more beautiful and will rejoice in your own being.

Your. . . . .

E., formerly, in his youth, a radical, and now an ardent Zionist, invited me, together with two more of his friends, to take a trip through the Arab village of Abu-Shusha, which nestles at the foot of the mountains of Judah. E. lives in London, but had been in Palestine for a short time. In partnership with a group of wealthy Russian Jews he has purchased a large tract of land near Abu-Shusha, and wishes to build a Jewish colony there.

Near the place where the Arab village now stands was once situated the city of Gezer, which is often mentioned in the Bible, as well as on the tablets that have been discovered in Tel el-Amarna. Of this Gezer it is recounted in Joshua that when the Jews entered Eretz Yisroel "they drove not out the Canaanites that dwelt in Gezer; but the Canaanites dwelt in the midst of Ephraim, unto this day, and became servants to do taskwork."

The road from Rehoboth led through gardens and fields, and on either side the eye was refreshed with sun-flooded verdure. Soon, however, the landscape became cheerless. The scene was half barren, the road became rocky and slippery, and the further we proceeded the rockier and more desolate it appeared. It was evident that human foot but rarely passed this way.

In certain spots the young Jewish Arabagi drove along at random, following no road at all, over stones and amidst rocks, and in order to keep from falling out, we had to hold tightly on to our places.

On the way there occurred a small incident that might have had serious consequences, had not all of us, with E. at our head, intervened in time.

This incident taught us how easily bloody clashes may arise between Jews and Arabs, on account of the carelessness or insolence of irresponsible individuals.

In order to avoid the stones, the driver, a half-Arabianized teamster of Eretz Yisroel, with a drayman's sense of fitness, drove upon a freshly ploughed area of land. An Arab, evidently the owner, noticed this from a distance, and shouted to him to get off the field. But instead of obeying, the driver began to curse the Arab in a loud voice, in the meantime driving further into the garden patches.

The Arab was incensed. He bent down hastily, seized a stone and dashed toward us. A few other Arabs, who, from adjoining fields, had witnessed the driver's spiteful action, likewise came running in our direction. They were all frightfully excited.

Who can tell what misfortune might have taken place, had not E. and the rest of us intervened? The driver simply insisted on driving straight ahead, and we were barely able by force to restrain him from doing so. The little Arabic that E. had learned during his short residence in Palestine proved most useful to him now. With the few words at his command spoken in a

"Zionist"accent, he managed to calm the excited Arabs, and the matter came to a peaceful conclusion.

I was heartily ashamed. In America a farmer, upon such provocation, would have used his rifle. And had he killed one of us, the jury would probably have acquitted him.

The nearer we came to the Judean mountains, the more they lost that nebulous, dreamy charm which they possess when viewed from one of the hills that encircle Rehoboth. The blue veil was rent asunder, and there were revealed gray, repulsive, scraggy ridges. We were face to face with ugly, drab reality.

At last we reached the site of ancient Gezer. On every hand were seen open ditches and heaps of earth —signs of the excavations carried on here by the famous Macalister, together with other English archeologists. These excavations were begun some time ago on a very large scale, and lasted several years. By unbaring stratum after stratum there appeared the traces of various peoples that had dwelt in different ages.

At first come the Horites of the Bible, who dwelt, as their name shows (Hor=hole,cave) in holes or caves. They lived here about five thousand years ago. About five hundred years later, when the Semites began to pour into Palestine, the Horites gave way to the Canaanites. Still later the kings of Egypt spread their rule and their Egyptian culture as far as Gezer.

A passage in Kings reads: "For Pharaoh king of Egypt had gone up, and taken Gezer, and burnt it with fire, and slain the Canaanites that dwelt in the city, and given it for a portion unto his daughter, Solomon's wife."

Clay documents that have been unearthed by the excavations show that the Egyptians never completely released Gezer from their clutches. The Egyptian princess did not have more than the income, and after her death the dowry was very neatly taken back.

We rode to Solomon's dowry. To-day even a humble father would be ashamed to give such a dot. It would be impossible to catch a doctor with such bait, that much is certain. And yet in those days, with such a worthless piece of property one could catch for a son-in-law the king of all the animals and fowls and spirits, and the author of such popular works as the Song of Songs—with the added stipulation, too, that after the bride's death the dowry would revert to her parents.

E. says, however, that the soil here is very fertile, and that which the Horites, the Canaanites, and the Pharaohs were not able to accomplish, he, with the aid of modern agriculture, will bring about.

We rode up a small hill, and entered Abu-Shusha—a typical Arabian village. The streets were narrow, tortuous, and the houses—or more exactly speaking, the kennels— were of clay without windows, huddled together as if in distrust of God's beautiful, sunny world, and bordered by piles of dung that had been accumulating through generations, while the fields round about lie fallow year after year, begging a hand-ful of manure.

Not that the heap of manure goes to waste. In the

Arab village the dung-heap takes the place of the turf-bench (Prizba) in Lithuania. Here the villagers gather to smoke and chat, or to stretch themselves and bask idly in the sun.

Our wagon barely managed to make its way through the narrow streets, until we were again out of the village. As it reached the summit of the mountain, it drove into a yard encircled by a thick stone wall, and stopped before a tall stone structure. We crawled down from the wagon, weary and broken up by the roughness of our journey.

The overseer, a neat young Arab, came forward to receive us, and after a friendly "marhaban" he led us to the second story, to a comfortable, well-kept room, which is held in continuous readiness for guests.

The stony coolness of the room was refreshing, after the hot rays that had been scorching us during the whole of our journey. Like an experienced traveller, E. had brought along provisions from the Rehoboth hotel. The young Arab prepared the table, and we sat down at once to our meal. In conclusion we drank black coffee, served, in Arab fashion, in diminutive cups.

All the time I felt as if I were in a medieval robber-baron's tower. The house, the thick wall surrounding it, and the seclusion, produced the impression rather of a stronghold than of a dwelling for ordinary people.

After we had finished our coffee we went out on the balcony, and saw before us the most glorious panorama that I have beheld in Eretz Yisroel. Before our eyes was spread the whole valley of Sharon in every variety

of gay color. Here was the colony of Ekron; there
Rehoboth, and farther still Rishon l'Zion. Yonder
in another direction, lay Ramleh of Crusaders' memory. There, too, was the pointed Minaret, and
there the cloister. And on the distant horizon a strip
of the Mediterranean Sea. The air was clear and
balmy. The landscape was gentle and restful, as if
created expressly for a life of contemplation and quiet.

As we sat on the balcony, E. told us the tale of
the remarkable structure and the thick wall. The
tale scarcely harmonized with the soft beauty of the
scene that lay before our eyes.

Years and years ago a German Jew came to Jerusalem. He had a hard time making both ends meet,
and suffered intense want, until one day he went off to
the missionaries and struck a bargain; a soul minus
Judaism in exchange for Christianity plus money.

Soon after his apostasy he was overwhelmed with
prosperity. And as soon as he had accumulated a tidy
sum, he became a usurer. He would lend money to the
Arab fellahin at exorbitant rates, taking their land as
collateral. Generally the debt and the interest would
grow and grow, until the land came into his hands.

In this manner he became the proprietor of a piece
of land in Abu-Shusha, where he settled in time. From
that point as his centre he wove his web like a spider,
to catch the surrounding Arabs, and sucked in all
their possessions. The fellahin hated him as a 'shaitan'
(devil), and writhed in his clutches.

So he decided to build a house here and make it as
strong and well-protected as possible. He knew that

the fellahin hated him fiercely. But in this stone fortress he could laugh their hate to scorn.

Nemesis, however, came to the apostate-usurer, not at all in connection with his extortion. It rather had to do with—a beautiful Arab girl, upon whom he had cast his eye or laid his hand.

One day a bullet from an Arab put an end to both his greed and his lust.

IMPATIENCE

Guests arrived, guests departed, yet we were still at the hotel. I became one of the household, with special privileges. I could allow myself, for example, the luxury to send for a cup of tea and cake at a time of day when ordinary guests were mightily pleased to be permitted to sleep. The hotel-keeper had to such an extent begun to consider me one of the family, that he even told me what a good season he had enjoyed that year. He planned to put up the following year a two-story modern hotel that would be an ornament to Rehoboth. The only trouble was that he could not procure a decent piece of land. All he needed was two dunam, and the wealthy Madame D. had a vast stretch of land that she had inherited from her husband years before. But no matter how much she was offered, she asked more, and when she was offered the sum that she herself had demanded, she would change her mind. Her children she kept abroad, while she remained here watching the land increase in price from year to year as a result of the colony's growth.

In the meantime the land lay idle, and nobody derived any benefit from it. Yet when you spoke to her, she assumed an attitude as one of the upbuilders of Rehoboth.

Despite this home-like feeling at the hotel, the life there grew daily more tedious to me. And just as a

pious Jew awaits the coming of the Messiah, even so
did I await the day when we should move into a home
of our own. As long as I remained at the hotel I was a
tourist, a foreigner, and I was anxious to settle down
and become a tax-paying citizen of the Moshevah.

More than anything else I was bored by the fact
that at every moment I'd have to supply another guest
with an answer to the question: Why didn't I journey
to Jerusalem, to the Mount of Olives, to the holy graves,
and so on? Of the numerous tourists that passed
through the hotel during my ten weeks' residence,
there was not one who could understand why I had
stowed myself away in a place like Rehoboth. Since
I did not intend to purchase a biareh or almond-grove
and did not mean to become a colonist, what sort of
place was Rehoboth for me?

Many of these tourists knew the trick of being
everywhere and seeing all the notable attractions of
Eretz Yisroel within a single week. For the most part
they were busy people—merchants, doctors, writers.
They did not have any too much time. They had
come for but a short holiday, and had to make a
"quick job" of it. Many of them, indeed, looked as if
they were driven to do a hard task.

Most in a hurry were the writers and journalists,
who had already capitalized in advance their impres-
sions of Palestine. The dailies and the journals were
eagerly watching for their books or articles, and the
type-setters were impatiently waiting for copy.

Wisest of all were those of whom it is told that they

had written their articles on shipboard, on their way to Jaffa.

I became so impatient that for days at a time I did not know what to do with myself. Every day I'd go to M. and bother him again, asking him to have compassion and step over to see the kalsominer. So he'd gather his courage and proceed to martyrdom. But he would always return downcast, and I would understand that he had been bawled out by the kalsominer's wife, and had barely escaped with his life.

Thus passed weeks and weeks, and I was already beginning to think that after all I'd be compelled to leave beautiful Rehoboth and seek my home elsewhere.

One day M. burst into my room panting with the glad tidings that we had won. The kalsominer's wife had capitulated. "She is ready to move."

I could barely restrain from embracing M. for joy. The eyes of both of us grew moist.

"As soon as—"

"As what?" I ask, and feel as if my nerves are collapsing with the presentiment of a horrible catastrophe.

"As soon as....as we'll find her another place."

"And you agreed?"

The bashful M. looks at me with his naive, blue eyes.

"She's is a lion, not a woman."

Whereupon all our friends set out to hunt up an apartment for the kalsominer. And we found one.

But we encountered a repetition of our own story. Every tenant said that he would move if another apartment were procured for him.

Half the colony grew interested in the matter, and within a few weeks our rooms, thank the Lord, were ready for us.

The long awaited day has come at last. Yesterday a huge old camel brought the household goods which we ordered from Jaffa. Apart from the fact that one side of a bed was broken, the transportation was successfully effected. At the same time I received the desk that I had ordered of a former editor of the "Wecker"—a good Yiddishist and an even better carpenter. God only knows how he has strayed to Tel-Aviv.

To-day I inscribed my name in the register of our hotel together with a generous litany of praises concerning the meals, the treatment, and so on. I took leave of the proprietor and the guests, upon whom I looked as a released prisoner looks at those whom he leaves behind in jail, and with a light, care-free heart went to our own home.

AMID TREES

No one asks me any longer why I do not go on a sight-seeing tour through Eretz Yisroel. I am now a full-fledged inhabitant of Rehoboth. When I speak of Rehoboth, I speak in the first person plural. I tell the Jews from Chicago that come to visit us that "our" orchards had a wonderful season this year, that "our" almond-groves are "doing fine," and "our" grapes are fair. The only trouble is that "we" lack land.

My little daughter goes to school now. The boycott which the children of Rehoboth at first declared against her, because she did not understand Hebrew, was gradually raised, and she has many friends. A few nights ago I received the best possible proof that Rehoboth did its work. She quarrelled in her sleep with a chum—in Hebrew.

Our house stands in the centre of a newly planted orchard. It contains many varieties of trees—apple, apricot, peach, almond, olive, palm, and orange, besides several bushes of Eve's figs—the Eretz Yisroel name for bananas.

Most of the trees are too young to bear fruit. But even I, who am far from an expert in horticulture, can see that in time they will be quite respectable trees. So I regard them betimes with the highest consideration.

Somewhat aloof from the saplings stands the venerable citron-tree and looks scornfully at the mere promise of their bare branches. It alone is laden with fruit. It is situated exactly opposite our dining-room, and when we sit down to tea, it thrusts a lemon-laden branch in through the open window.

"Bevakkashah!"

We can't refuse, even though the citrons are still green. Moreover, we mustn't postpone our acceptance, for the lame blacksmith that lives behind our house does not wait for an invitation from the tree. He has a prior right to the tree, dating from before our arrival.

The lame blacksmith, however, is not totally devoid of consideration. So that from time to time he presents us with a bunch of the bananas that grow near his smithy.

The girls of the school likewise have a prior right to the flowers that grow around our house. They refuse to be driven away. Day after day we catch them pluck-ing the white, red, and yellow roses, often before the petals have had a chance to open fully. If we chase them away, they return bright and early next morning, tearing off as many as they can before we run out to defend our property.

Part of the dark red roses I use as messengers. When I send a letter to a friend across the seas I enclose a few petals. They are fresh when I put them in, and will be withered when they arrive, but something of the fragrance will remain and find its way into someone's heart.

Our house has large windows on every side. The windows are always open. The glorious light pours in and spreads golden carpets over the high white walls and the tiled floor, not overlooking the tiniest nook.

From dawn to dusk the house is filled with chirping and twittering. Birds fly in through one window and out through another. They play hide-and-seek, and cut all sorts of capers, hovering right above our heads, as if they, not we, were the proprietors. They, too, from the looks of things, have a prior right. Since I hung up the Mogen David, woven of new corn-ears and presented to me by Khawaja Musa, in honor of the festival of First Fruit (Shebu'oth), my room has become a veritable rendezvous for all the birds in Eretz Yisroel.

The mischievous little creatures at once scented its presence, and from every direction they came to me unbidden for dainties. A peck at a corn, a tweet-tweet which in Eretz Yisroel means "Lehitraot" (See you again!), a dash through the window, and the marauder disappears.

And thus things went on day after day, until the Mogen David was left empty, mere husks. Not a single grain was overlooked.

The days pass by quietly, sunny and pregnant with growth, one by one. The outside world is curtained from my view on every side by green trees. The sky is blue day after day, week after week.

There will be no more rain till Heshvan. Now and then a cloud appears, grows denser and darker, and spreads angrily over the sky. At any moment, it seems, the world will be deluged. But I know that this is merely a hoax.

And the certainty of sunny days for months and months in succession instils into the soul a feeling of security.

Everything now lives on the bounty of the skies. The oranges receive their gold, the almonds ripen their kernels, and the grapes fill up—and all this is the work of the sun.

In Eretz Yisroel the sky is more important than the earth. The chief nourishment seems to come from above.

At twilight there often come heavy, melancholy hours. The sun gathers its last remnants of light, and carries it over our orchard, into our yard behind the house, and the last rays creep thence away, across the gardens. A bird pauses opposite the window and utters piercing staccato sounds, summoning from somewhere desolate, weird images.

When I come over to the furthermost window of the house, the sun has already set behind a wall of cypresses, that rise sharp and black against the flaming sky.

Boecklin's "Isle of the Dead". All at once I feel sundered from the rest of the world, forsaken, as if marooned upon a desert-island in mid-ocean.

SERVANT GIRLS

Everyone in the colony has a Yemenite servant girl. Even the poor instructor of the school-house has one. The meagre wages he receives do not permit him to maintain a grown-up one, so he has to be content with a tot of about six or seven, and thus keep up appearances.

As soon as we moved into our own home and set up housekeeping, we realized that we could not get along without a Yemenite servant. Not so much because of the work there was to be done, as for the sake of our "reputation". A fine name we'd make for ourselves in Rehoboth if we didn't have a Yemenite girl in the house!

The first "girl" we took into the house, upon the recommendation of an acquaintance, was a widow with sad eyes and a small, thin countenance, as brown and wrinkled as a well-baked apple. She looked as old as eternity, although according to the number of her years she was far from being an aged woman. In the lands of the east old age comes soon.

It was quite evident that she had not left Yemen so long ago, for she spoke only her mother-tongue, Arabic. She did not know a word of Hebrew. So that we could use her for only such work as we could assign to her by deaf-and-dumb language. She appeared so starved and slavishly submissive that it pained one to look at her. And she would be continually saying: "Kathar Herak" (May your weal increase, i. e., Thanks), and kissing your hand.

She felt the deepest respect particularly for me and for my room. For this consideration I had to thank the book-case that stood in the corner, and, even more, the heavy-paunched Standard Dictionary that lay upon the table.

Whenever she happened to pass the table, she would never fail to bend over and reverentially kiss the dictionary.

She was followed by Shama, a tall, bony young woman, who worked herself to death so as to support her husband, the *hakham*. She would come to us for half a day only. The rest of the time she worked at the school and at the "town hall". She was the *hakham's* second wife. The first he had cast aside when she had grown too old for him. I used to see him often when I stayed at the hotel. His shop was in the cellar of the hotel. He was an armorer, and the Bedouins of the vicinity would come to him to have their weapons repaired. He would squat upon the ground exposing his bare feet. All his time would be spent in hunting for his tools, which were scattered in confusion in every corner of the cellar. His every second phrase would be "Blessed be the holy Name". If he found his wrench, "Blessed be the holy Name." If he lost his wrench and found his little hammer, "Blessed be the holy Name". If he lost both and found a screw, once again "Blessed be the holy Name." If an abundance of work happened to accumulate, he would rise to his feet in the midst of it all, leave everything to God's tender mercies and stride off barefoot to Jaffa on some matter or other, "Blessed be the holy Name", that he had to discuss with the *hakham* of that city.

One day we had a fright on account of him. We were sitting at the table when suddenly we heard a rifle shot, and at the same time a cry from the *hakham* in the cellar.

We dashed down and found the *hakham* writhing in pain, his hand bathed in blood. An Arab had left a rifle with him to be repaired, and had forgotten to remove the bullets. The *hakham* had come near shooting off a finger during the repairing. He went off to the doctor to have his injured member bandaged, and there was no more thought of work. In the colony there were found persons hard-hearted enough to believe that the whole episode had been nothing but a scheme of the *hakham's*. He had simply become weary of work.

Our third experiment was named Shoshannah (Lily), and was an exception. And when I say an exception, this is what I mean.

I have no statistics to adduce in proof of my statement, but my own observation was that the more beautiful a Yemenite woman's name was the uglier she was herself.

Our Shoshannah did not belong to this category. She was really a beautiful, well-developed young woman of about eighteen, such as is seldom encountered among the Yemenites, and did not disgrace her name.

She had been married twice. The first time, she had stepped under the wedding canopy at the age of eight. Even now she would have been dwelling in peace and joy with her first beloved, for they both loved each other. Yet they were divorced, against the will of both. It was none other than the British government that was to blame. As ill-fortune would have it, her husband was registered as a British subject. A former wife of his, an old woman of twenty, whom he had abandoned for his new mate, lodged a complaint with the English consul, and on the strength of the English law against bigamy she forced the newly-wedded pair to be divorced.

Shoshannah was one of the most industrious creatures in the world. She simply wearied us with her insatiable demand for work. In an hour or two she would complete every household duty, and then she would stand with her arms crossed against her bosom like a tax-collector: More work. She spoke excellent Yiddish, but was always scolding my wife for not learning Hebrew.

Her second husband, a handsome man of twenty-five, who wore his turban askew, like a dandy, was a Shomer. In addition to this, they both had another source of income. They were the musicians at the Yemenite weddings. She was employed for the women, he for the men. Their instrument was the cymbal with the iron clapper.

She was as if created specially for our needs, only that we were soon infected by acquaintances with the suspicion that she did not believe in private property, particularly when she saw it lying loose about the house.

Our fourth was Esther. She was a small-built di-
vorcee of about twenty-five or six. Green and ugly as
death. Since she had no father, her wages—according
to the Yemenite custom—were taken by her own
brother.

She came to us from Ben-Shemen. And because of
that, she did not stay very long. She kept complaining
that she was lonesome in our house. In Ben-Shemen
the workingmen would sing such merry songs and
dance such pretty rounds, while in our home all was
as silent as in a grave-yard.

Often, in the midst of her labors, she would disappear. After a long search she would be found somewhere in the rear of the house sitting on the scorching
sand, with her legs spread out wide, broiling in the
sun. Otherwise she was a fine servant, and as honest
as the day. But Ben-Shemen took her away from us.

She lost her appetite entirely, would refuse to
take food. Her eyes were forever filled with tears,
until one day she disappeared, and returned no more.

"EL-KUDS ESH-SHERIF"

I was sitting one morning upon the stone porch overlooking our orchard. From across the way, on the other side of the orchard, came the clear, shrill sounds of the young instructress marching her tiny army around the kindergarten and counting their steps.

"Ahat, Shtayim; Ahat, Shtayim."

From another direction were wafted the voices of the older school children singing; "Sweet it is to dwell in our land", in tones that made up in lusty, full-throated power what they lacked in harmonic charm.

From behind the house came the resounding blows of our neighbor's heavy hammer falling rhythmically upon the anvil, and from the other side of the synagogue somebody was answering: Tang, tang.

Above, from a near-by cote, a flock of white pigeons took to flight, spreading like white blossoms against the clear sky.

I sat there watching a long black caravan of ants approaching from a distant field, winding around the porch and centring upon the young apricot tree. Those who returned were laden with all manner of good things: wisps of straw, splinters, strips of leaves, and they hastened to hide their booty and return for more.

All at once out of the light and the surrounding peacefulness stalked a huge gray object and asked:

"Why have you forgotten me? From distant lands and over vast seas have you come, and yet your eyes do not wish to behold me".

Between me and the tender saplings of our garden stood and wept a dark stone wall—the Wailing Wall.

And as the days grew longer, the heavy stones weighed upon my heart, and the gray object pursued me: "Why do you slight me?"

I was wont to say to myself that a single orchard planted by Jewish hands was more important than all the graves of the House of David; that a single foundation dug is worth a hundred crumbling ruins. But the huge gray object persecuted me like a demon, and would give me no rest.

So I decided to take a trip to Jerusalem and see the *Kotel ha-Ma'arabi.*

Mahmud came again and drove us to Ramleh. In Ramleh we took the train to El-Kuds. The small compartment was crowded with people. In one corner sat two elderly Jews from Jerusalem, with fur-caps and gabardines, and curly ear-locks that dangled down to their chins. Opposite them was a German who seemed to be an old Palestinian settler. The two elderly Jews got into a conversation with the German about Austria. They spoke a really excellent German. They were evidently business men before they came to spend their declining years in the holy city.

Not far from them sat a Russian pilgrim in a heavy long coat and a fur hat, cutting off tiny slices of orange with a rusty knife. These he would place carefully into his mouth, eating them together with huge pieces of black bread.

The rest of the car was filled with Arabs, among them some soldiers who smoked continuously, and sang melancholy songs. The train moved along in leisurely fashion, and the rhythmic whir of the wheels furnished a gloomy accompaniment to their sad tunes. One of them, in a half-tearful, chanting voice, would sing a verse, whereupon the rest would join in chorus, uttering long, protracted nasal sounds:

"Ya ha-sa-ra-ti (O woe is me)."

I looked through the window. The landscape through which we were journeying—the ancient battlefield of the Jews against the Philistines—was gray, parched, and desolate. The hills were colorless and unattractive. From station to station the scenery grew more and more dreary and desert-like, more forsaken and accursed.

I closed my eyes, and soon there rose before me a desolate stone wall:

"Ya ha-sa-ra-ti."

The train began to pant its way up-hill, and made its first stop, to catch its breath for a few minutes, at Bittir, a pretty little village, which in no way recalled the great ancient Bethar that was the scene of Bar-Kochba's exploits.

The desolation and dreariness ceased. A hand was stretched out: thus far and no farther.

The landscape became green and fertile. On both sides rose terrace upon terrace, beautifully cultivated, well-plotted gardens. The nearer we approached the city, the fresher, greener, and more beautiful became the scene.

Jerusalem! We arrived at twilight, as the last golden rays fell upon the minarets and spires of the holy city.

Sharp, slender silhouettes rose darkly against the clear, fiery heavens, while from the surrounding mountains descended shadows that glided through the streets.

A carriage brought us to the house of P. an instructor in painting at the Bezalel School, where we had been invited to spend the night. Early next morning, P. promised that he would take us to the Wailing Wall.

I scarcely closed my eyes all night, and about six in the morning I woke my little family, as well as the congenial P. Half an hour later we were already out of the house.

On the way P. told me how he had come from Paris, where he had forsaken a brilliant career, and how the old city had cast its spell over him. His eyes could not see enough of it, and his heart was intoxicated.

The street was still bathed in the cool morning light. Yet despite the early hour, there was plenty of stir. For the most part it was children on their way to school or heder.

We went through the Jaffa gate, which used to be closed every night. Close by this gate the Sultan Abdul Hamid had an entrance broken through the city wall in honor of Kaiser Wilhelm, when the latter visited Jerusalem in 1898.

There is an old Mohammedan tradition that no Christian ruler may enter through the gates of "El-Kuds Esh-Sherif" (Sublime Holiness) either on horseback or in carriage, and in order that the "Protector of Islam" might not have to enter on foot, a breach was made in the wall for his special benefit.

We went down hill through narrow lanes and dark, arched passages, and came to a small path of steps. Round about, as far as the eye could reach, was filth and poverty.

I followed P. in a sort of gray, heavy daze. I was hardly able to see or make out anything.

"Here is the Wall."

P.'s voice woke me up. Before me rose a bare, lofty stone wall. At the bottom there were rows of huge, massive, square stones with the characteristic hewn edges from the time of the second temple. Above, the stones were smaller, and of later date.

It was yet too early for visitors and for the beggars who come to seek alms. Of these latter there were but half a dozen in all. With the exception of our party, there were no visitors.

An elderly Jew stood leaning against a stone, weeping over a book of Psalms. A woman half lay, half sat in a corner upon the ground, reciting, in a chant that had become mechanical with frequent repetition, the prayer "Gate of Tears". Another woman, a Sephardith, was running up and down close to the wall, as if crazy, murmuring a prayer in Spanish. I could catch only the words: 'Senor del mundo, Senor grande" (Lord of the Universe, great God), which she kept on repeating. Every moment she would place her lips impulsively against a stone and kiss it passionately.

In many places the stones had been worn smooth— the effect of hundreds of thousands of lips that had kissed the cold rock in the course of centuries.

Iron nails have been placed in the fissures between the stones. This has been done for some superstitious purpose. Some people throw prayer slips into the fissures, with requests inscribed upon them. God in heaven alone knows how many sorrowful supplications are thus lying around in the dark fissures.

Six Jews, some of them mere youngsters, in long coats and with exceedingly long ear-locks, arrived, and at once began to recite Psalms in a very loud voice. They were evidently hired mourners. Upon their faces were all the marks of the professional Kaddish-reciter.

A woman entered all at once, fell against a stone, and began to sob and wail as if over a dead body. Somebody was ill or at death's door, so she had come to knock at the last gate.

From minute to minute her plaints grew louder and more heart-breaking. An old Jew approached her, and began to solace her in a low voice, but she did not cease weaping and sobbing.

A woman whom the weeper was disturbing in her devotions began to scold her, and even as she scolded, she herself burst into bitter tears.

My eyes were dry, but my heart overflowed with tears—of sadness? No! of bitterness and humiliation. My glance, with a strange sort of self-torture, was glued to the wailing, unhappy woman who stood moaning against the stone.

From her throat issued the sob of a down-trodden race that had come to knock at the last gate. My little daughter was on the verge of tears. The old woman had frightened her. Her youthful freshness was out of keeping with this wailing and the ancient ruins.

From between the fissures of the stone came crawling forth, like a tortoise, the legend:

Once upon a time, hundreds and hundreds of years ago, a new sultan arrived in Jerusalem. He was a gracious king, and wished to build up the city anew. So he had a large number of houses and palaces reared, and in one of the palaces he himself took up his residence.

One morning, gazing out of the palace window, as was his wont, he noticed an old woman horribly bent beneath the burden of a huge basket filled with dung. With her last atom of strength she managed to carry the basket to a hill not far from the sultan's palace, and there she emptied it. The sultan sent one of his servants after the woman. When she came before him, he asked her how she dared to cast dung near the sultan's palace.

The old woman fell prostrate before his feet and answered: "O great king, it is not my fault. It has been enjoined upon us from generation to generation. When Titus brought my ancestors hither from Rome, he commanded that they and their children and their children's children cast their dung upon the spot where the Temple had stood. So we obey his command to this very day."

Whereupon the sultan issued an order to have the hill of dung removed, and for months and months they kept digging until the Wailing Wall was excavated.

When the spot had been totally cleaned, the sultan sent for the Rabbis and the elders of Jerusalem, and told them to build anew the Temple in all its pristine glory. Whereupon the Rabbis and the elders bowed low before the sultan, thanking him for the great favor that it had pleased him to bestow, but entreated him to let the Wailing Wall stand as it was, and all they asked was the privilege of coming every Friday night to weep before the old stones.

No one was permitted to hasten the hour of redemption. . .

ON THE WAY BACK

The stone wall had produced a gloomy impression upon me, and I was anxious to return to beautiful, verdant Rehoboth in all haste. I wanted to shake off as quickly as possible the cold, dead ruins, and once again fill my lungs with the fragrant atmosphere of the vineyards.

Before leaving, we made a short visit to the Bezalel. There was not much to see. In the metal department a few Yemenites were working at filigree. The other departments were nearly or entirely empty. Professor Borris Schatz was at that time in America with his exposition, seeking to raise sufficient funds to pay off the debts and continue the shaky Bezalel.

At last P. took us into his drawing class.

On a low platform in the forward part of the room sat an aged Yemenite with a long, snow-white beard; before him, with their faces turned toward him, were seated, in various corners, some twenty youths and maidens. Before each of these students stood an easel and a sheet upon which they were drawing the old man. They were all deeply engrossed in their work, though they were not all equally successful.

The hired patriarch fulfilled faithfully every duty of a model, and did not move a muscle. He certainly earned in honest, upright fashion the fee of a few francs that he gets from Bezalel for his patriarchal posing.

During the time that P. went from stand to stand, looking over the work of his pupils, I scrutinized the old man. His tiny, shrewd eyes were filled with a world of mockery. He was studying the sketchers far more than the pupils were studying him, and evidently entertained no very high opinion of them.

In *Ka'a al-Yahud* in Sana he certainly had never dreamed that he would make his living from such mad people.

As we passed through a corridor, I caught a glimpse, through a tiny window in a closed door, of a dust-laden bird's head. This was the zoological collection that Ahroni had gathered at the cost of so much effort and patience, during the time he had been connected with the Bezalel Institute. Now the room is closed. There is nobody to care for the birds and animals. So the dust gathers from year to year, and the collection that was assembled with such hard work is crumbling into decay.

Jerusalem is more than two thousand feet above sea-level, and the air is most invigorating, but I must confess that I breathed easier when our train began to roll down the hill on the road to Jaffa. My impatience to reach home grew with every minute. I was afraid to look back, lest I should behold behind me that dark wall and that dust-laden bird with the round, glassy eyes in pursuit of me.

We arrived at Jaffa about noon. We hired a carriage and left the station at once for Tel-Aviv, where

I wished to spend the couple of hours that would elapse before the coach left for Rehoboth, incidentally tasting the fare of our former boarding-house.

Every time I visit Tel-Aviv I find new buildings. The appearance of the beautiful suburb keeps changing continually, and may I be pardoned if I say that every time I come it seems to me that not only have the streets changed in looks, but that the chaste beauty, which once marked Tel-Aviv, is gradually paling, disappearing.

From an educational centre, Tel-Aviv is little by little being transformed into a town of villas, a tourist resort where people come to spend a few pleasant days or weeks. Wherever you turn there is either a restaurant or a hotel. One feels it in the air that the town is on the look-out for the tourists.

About three o'clock we went to the "khan", whence the Rehoboth coach leaves for that place. The coach was filled to capacity—nine, three in a row—and set out. As it left, it came near running over the Arab blacksmith, who could find no better site for his smithy than the very middle of the gateway. Every time we leave by that same entrance, the same accident occurs. The Arab blacksmith is almost run over. A hue and cry is raised, the blacksmith utters a volley of curses in his own tongue upon the head of Ahmed, and Ahmed replies with every name in the catalogue of abuse. The passengers raise a commotion, and the asses in the khan bray in unison—until the coach finally drives into the street.

In addition to Rehobothans returning home, we had with us a 'new face': a maiden—one of those Zionist-Hebraists of the kind in whom eagerness to find a husband is so closely intertwined with interest in the settlement and in the "renaissance of the language", that is difficult to tell what is nut and what is shell.

She is—I soon learn—a Hebrew instructress from somewhere in the vicinity of Vilna, and arrived in company of a young group—all of them teachers, who came to spend their vacation in excursions through Judea and Galilee. They are now on the way to Rehoboth, and as she is behind time, she is trying to catch up with them by taking the coach.

She spoke Hebrew in very ostentatious fashion, and the young overseer of T.'s orchard, who never in his life had cause to call himself anything other than Mendelovitch, she promptly began to address as Ben-Menahem.

She tells me that she was at the last Zionist Congress, and enumerates all the "big people" she has seen there. She was even fortunate enough to speak with some of them, with the American delegates, for example. Since she knows that I come from America, she asks me whether I have ever enjoyed the good fortune of speaking with the afore-mentioned celebrities.

I answer "Yes". But the girl suspects me. Americans are known for their "bluff".

Not far from Vadi Khanin we caught up with the tourists. The poor pedagogues were very tired from trudging up to the ankles in sand, but they strode heroically forward, infusing, every other moment, courage into their hearts with a Hebrew song.

By the time we had aproached Rehoboth it was quite dark, and the night fell moist and heavy upon the valley. Not far from the road some Bedouins were setting fire to heaps of dry grass. Every moment the flames would leap into the air, and against the red flames would appear the silhouettes of figures in loose cloaks, seated in a circle, and women bent over, stirring large, dark pots with their long, thin hands. Above the heads of all hovered a dense smoke wreathing itself into the strangest forms.

When the ruddy flames leaped higher, they would reveal behind them the black tents, surrounded by camels with outstretched necks. And here and there the pointed head of a shepherd-dog would be seen.

"A JEWISH STATE"

Dear . . . .

I'll surely be flayed if it is discovered that I read Herzl's *Judenstaat* for the first time only after having settled in Rehoboth. And by accident, at that. But it gave me deep, intense pleasure. The naive daring of the book is so refreshing, so heartening. There before you is a man, building in and of the air, with as much earnestness and certainty as if he felt the granite blocks in his hand.

Herzl did not possess the Jewish acumen, the analytical mind which tears things to pieces, and therein lies his greatness and the secret of his leadership. This very over-keenness that we have developed in our exile life, just as the cactus has grown its spines, and the porcupine its bristles, and the rattle-snake its rattlers—for the purpose of protection against a hostile external world—this over-keenness we shall lose in Eretz Yisroel. The soil will absorb our excessive acumen, and we shall be the healthier for it.

When Herzl came, and with a wave of his hand thrust aside all our rationalness, our timorousness, we sensed the redeemer and the leader in him, for our rationalness had corroded our souls like rust, and we despised ourselves, because we knew that it was the fruit of our fear and weakness, and would lead to decadence.

The author of the *Judenstaat* was a piece of Eretz Yisroel transformed into flesh and blood. All the sappy odor of the Eretz Yisroel soil rises from his printed words—the unity and the vigor, the healing, restorative power of that soil. The great new word that he brought us, which shall prove our salvation, is this: we must cease being over-wise.

He was a builder and a creator, and what he created and did was of one piece. We have had false builders. They were builders by error. They were originally meant to be dissectors, and when fate spitefully made them constructors, the cracks and the defects were everywhere discernible. He was the born builder and architect of unity. Of timid prudence and of argumentative questioning and cavilling he knew nothing, nor cared to know.

.   .   .   .

Now ask no more opinions of me. I am too biased to be a witness. If I have not already grown into Eretz Yisroel, Eretz Yisroel has grown into me. I see, or more exactly speaking, I sense everything from within. I breathe it, I thrive on it, I have it in my bones and feel that it can't be otherwise.

There is a festive Eretz Yisroel—a dress-parade, shouting "hedod"—and there is an every-day, hard-working, sound Eretz Yisroel. The first is for the tourists and the shekel-contributors who come to see what becomes of their shekels (I have known one who came to see *his* tree in the Herzl forest). The second reveals itself only to him who dwells close to it, to its intimates.

I am pleased that the atmosphere of holiness is disappearing. The pioneer in Eretz Yisroel must cease to regard himself as a martyr to whom every newcomer owes praise and recognition, and must cease to accompany the planting of every tree with "I am ready and prepared to perform the duty."* The reform is by no means completed. There is still more talk than action, and the argumentative thumb works harder than the hand. And there are some who are neither Sabbath nor week-day Jews—older idealists still bearing traces of their faded idealism. They give one the impression of a frayed satin coat, or of a very rare wine—become vapid.

. . . Whenever I get moody, I turn the version about and say: We have a wonderful land, and when the land is acquired, the proper persons will appear. The soil will produce them.

It is still early. We live now on the spiritual capital that we have brought along with us, and when in the course of the years the capital is used up, we are left poor, and are apt to take our cue from the Arabs. But I look upon everything as a promissory note, and the note is secure.

. . . You and I often used to sit together and say: Woe unto us that are born in an age of weakness, when the truth would often mean treachery. And we would dream of a time when we would be able to indulge with a good conscience in the pleasure of self-criticism.

Here, at last, the fear will disappear. The hoops are securely fastened, and should one rotten stave be thrown away, there will be no danger to the vessel.

*A prayer formula before performing a religious rite.

And now let me tell you of a visit I made: On a white quiet moonlit night I took a walk over to the working-men's club.

As I left the eucalyptus grove on the way that leads to the club, I could make out the small house from a distance, brightly lighted up, and a confusion of merry voices, laughing and singing, blended with the moonlight and spread over the whole valley.

I climbed the little hill, and entered the club. The room was filled with a hungry crowd. The co-operative buffet was besieged, and the attendant, a young man with a pair of earnest, melancholy eyes, could not hand out the desired dainties, bread, tea, and oranges, quickly enough. Those who had already bought their suppers were seated on long benches that were ranged around the large banquet table and were eating with such holiday gusto as if a royal feast lay before them.

I asked the quiet workingman at the buffet whether there were any other things on sale beside tea, oranges, and bread.

"We have", he answered, "herring a-plenty. But not everybody can afford it.

"And butter?" I asked, like a country gawk.

"There are certain tales going the rounds about butter."

A young man of about nineteen—a husky chap whose acquaintance I made a few days previous—caught sight of me, and came over to shake my hand.

"What shall I do about my appetite?"

"Lost it?" I asked, compassionately.

"No such luck," he laughed, showing his white teeth, which could have chewed up a horse-shoe. "It's growing from day to day. Once upon a time a loaf of bread at five *metalliks* was enough. Now *it*—meaning his sinful appetite—"demands a loaf and a half. Nothing less. That means a total of seven and a half *metalliks*. And *metalliks*, I'll have you understand, are with workingmen in Eretz Yisroel rather often conspicuous by their absence."

In the meantime the young fellow has swallowed his final morsel and begins to sing. The crowd chimes in, and the room resounds with singing and clapping of hands:

Boruch Eloheinu Shebro'onu Likhvodo,
Boruch Eloheinu Shebro'onu Likhvodo
　　Oy, Likh—vo—do.
La—dee—dee—, La—dee—da,
La—dee—dee—dom—dom.

I wondered what would have happened if I had suddenly interrupted their song and begun to read them Rosenfeld's well-known poem:

"Bread and tea, only bread and tea—
That is the fare of misery."

They would have torn me to pieces. The workingman with the sinful appetite would have been the first to order me thrown out. For the eater of bread and tea knows that he is the builder and the heir of the land.

As long as they were merely playing at Eretz Yisroel, and it was a luxury, the worthy, dignified, respectable people were sufficient. But now that the settlement had become the great, serious cause of the people, it was the workers' turn.

The orchard and the vineyard were after all no sweat shops. The blue sky and the sun made up with a lavish hand the deficit of the wages paid up by "Boaz". Moreover, "Boaz" has sacrificed a great deal and suffered much for the sake of Eretz Yisroel, and was bound to it by all the ties of his soul. And this joint love for the land and the people was far stronger and greater than the accounts between them.

Your............

"HIT'AHDUT HA-MOSHEVOT"
(ASSOCIATION OF THE COLONIES)

I took a trip to Rishon l'Zion with a few other members of the Rehoboth community, to attend a meeting of the Association of the Colonies, which had been founded not long before, and of which many practical accomplishments were expected for the settlement.

The meeting was held in the town hall, a high, spacious room with large windows on all sides. There were delegates from Petach Tikvah, Ekron, Gederah, Kastinieh, Be'er Ya'akov, Vadi Khanin, Rehoboth, and other colonies. The majority of them were men well advanced in years, some of them totally white-haired. They were all deepy-rooted inhabitants of Eretz Yisroel, whose probationary years were now far in the past —all of them representatives of the sound, growing settlement.

The session lasted, with a few recesses, a long time— about six hours. Those who took part in it displayed a wide acquaintance with affairs and a very practical spirit. Jewish brains appeared here in their most favorable light.

Many important questions were discussed. Among other things on the order of the day was the plan to issue a newspaper that would be the official organ of the colonists and furnish them, in addition to news and reading matter, useful information about agriculture, plantations, cattle-breeding, and so on.

The problem of an insurance company to cover cattle came up for discussion. During the consideration of the plan some of the delegates revealed an intimacy with the subject that could hardly have been expected from persons who had spent the greater part of their lives in a colony in Eretz Yisroel.

More than any other thing, they discussed the problem of neutralizing the anti-Jewish agitation being carried on by the Arab newspapers, and especially how to inform Jewish colonists as to what their Arab neighbors were thinking and saying about them.

This is the proper place to remak that the ignorance of the Jewish settlers in Palestine concerning the inner life and psychology of the Arabs is one of the weakest points of the settlement. Colonists who have been living in Eretz Yisroel for decades know only sufficient Arabic to converse with their Arab "Arabagi", or their Arab help. As to writing and reading Arabic, that is out of the question.

When an official order arrives from the government or even an ordinary Arabic document, there is often not a person in the colony who can make it out. There have been instances of persons signing papers that they never would have signed had they known what was written therein, and, as a consequence, there was much trouble.

The windows were open, and during the whole time that the meeting lasted, the birds did not cease to twitter from every direction. The chirping was so shrill that often we could not hear the speaker distinctly. To the thoughts that came to me, as I sat

amidst the assembled members, the merry mischief of
the birds and the sunniness of the hall furnished the
most appropriate of accompaniments.

"From just such a body as this", I said to myself,
"there will in time develop the first sound kernel of a
Jewish autonomous citizenship."

After the period of heroic pioneerdom would come
a time of courageous, proud citizendom, when the
William Tells would be born.

The program of the association is a vast and imposing one. It could be seen at once that not all the members were satisfied to have the organization concern
itself with matters other than agriculture and similar
immediate needs of the colonies.

It occurred to me that under the leadership of a few
broad-minded, capable, energetic spirits the organization could in time become the strongest in the land.
If it should be necessary to make the first attempt to
organize the diverse elements of Eretz Yisroel into
a single powerful union—and there can be no difference
of opinion on that score—then certainly the most sens-
ible course would be to begin with the colonists, who
are more bound to the land than the city-dwellers,
and are really the foundation-stones of the settlement.

While the meeting was still going on, I went out to
take a look at the colony.

An old, distinguished-looking colonist led me to the
park. The gate was closed—it is open only on Saturday, rarely during the week. My guide sent for the
key and invited me to enter. The park had several ave-
nues of glorious palm-trees, in addition to various

rare tropical trees. Part of the park was an orange-grove that added a yearly income of ten thousand francs to the community coffers.

The palms infused in me a particular pleasure. I often remarked to my acquaintances that in none of the Jewish colonies I had seen thus far had I met with a palm-tree—the most beautiful adornment of the Oriental landscape. The reason was not far to seek. Palms require years to grow, and the first persons to settle in the colony could not think of such luxuries as palms. There were more important things to worry about, and more urgent wants to supply.

In Rishon l'Zion there was evidently somebody at the very beginning who had an eye and a feeling for beauty, nor was the necessary money lacking. Baron Edmond de Rothschild gave with a lavish hand. Now the palms raise their heads high and proudly—a symbol of the past and its traditions.

Rishon l'Zion possesses another souvenir of the Baron—the wine-cellars, only part of which the colony-syndicate uses.

Then there is machinery to make ice enough for an entire country, yet Rishon l'Zion must do without ice. The machine is too large, and it doesn't pay to run it. I saw gigantic steel wheels and boilers rusting in their places. One boiler, when it arrived from France, was too huge to be put upon a bark. So it was framed in wood and sent floating down to the bank. And then it took days before it was transported to Rishon l'Zion over the soft, sandy road. Now the iron giant lies rusting. This gigantic scale, planned in Paris, came near crushing the settlement.

On our way back from Rishon l'Zion to Rehoboth, someone told a tale of how a commission from the Italian government had come to study the Jewish methods of colonization, so as to utilize them in Tripoli. A bouquet for our pioneers.

The night was pretty well advanced, and the sky was all stars.

By day the sun of Palestine broods over everything, and sucks in all thoughts and dreams. He draws them forth from their hiding-places, and they rise and evaporate in his brightness. Only with the glimmer of the stars do they return to reassert themselves and become free once again.

I say to myself: The prophets must have beheld all their visions by night. Eretz Yisroel is too bright by day.

A BIAREH

It is early Saturday morning. The school is closed, and the colony is quieter than usual. From the synagogue on the hill the cantor can be heard singing "Kedushah". The smithy to the rear of our house is closed, and the door is barred by a half-completed wheel. The limping smith has bedecked himself in his white, embroidered smock, and has gone with his young wife for a stroll to the small vineyard in which he invests everything that he can spare from his meagre earnings.

My neighbor Khawaja Musa calls me for a walk to his orange-grove. We pass by vineyards, through a grove of eucalypti, and proceed over the fields into the valley.

I look for my favorites, the yellow daisies and the wild, red anemones. But there is no longer a trace of them.

This is the time for matters more serious than flowers. The almonds are ripening and the grapes are swelling with wine. Labor and industry must reap their rewards

We reach the orchard. Stretched out on the bare soil near his house sleeps the watchman—a tall, thin, lanky Gurji in a thick coat, with empty, half-torn cartridge pockets on his breast and a black, Astrakhan hat, despite the fact that the sun is as hot as fire. Near his bare feet a gray, lean dog, which looks like a jackal, blinks in the sun.

The watchman wakes.

"Shabbat Shalom!"

"Shabbat Shalom!"

It is hot, so he fetches us an *ibrik* of cold water.

We walk silently through the rows of many-branched, low orange-trees. From the dark-green, umbrageous mass, bronze-hued, half-ripe oranges sparkle in the sun. The firm trunk gathers all its strength so as to support the heavy burden. Very often it must be aided. The wealth is too great. The branches droop under their precious load, and must be propped up by poles. Branches, leaves, trunk, and fruit are all occupied with a single purpose—growth. The roots suck and draw in the water that the *birke* sends to them through iron pipes and ask for more and more.

We go from one row to the next. Everywhere the same dense, firm, serious trees, engrossed in but a single concern, a single labor—to grow and produce as great an abundance as possible. We walk among them, and they nod to us with their green heads.

Sh–sh! We must not idle.

Khawaja Musa gazes lovingly upon his trees.

"Come, I'll show you the beginning."

He walks ahead, and I follow. We don't speak a word. We might, heaven forbid, disturb the orange-trees in their work.

We reach the extreme boundary of the orange-grove. Here is the "school" where the slips of sweet citron are nurtured. The sweet citron itself is of no value, but it produces the juicy delicious oranges. The good-for-nothing citron is taken out of the "school" and planted in good, rich soil. Then it is cuddled and tended, and when it has taken root and has become a denizen of its new home, its breast is cut open and a graft of an orange is inserted. The graft sucks in the sap of the futile citron, and lets out a shoot. This means the end of the citron, which is lopped off above the new twig. The heir grows and thrives, and the step-father is forgotten.

The citron, however, would not give in, and sprouts from underneath. But its efforts are chopped off. The sap must not be wasted. The orange nursling must have every drop. One single shoot only is permitted to survive. It is food for the tree. The Arabs call this solitary offspring of the citron-tree 'khinzir' (pig).

We leave the orchard. The sky dazzles with its blueness, and the landscape is white with sunshine.

"You know," my companion says, "sometimes I long for snow. The Russian frost and the white fields often come to my mind, and the soul yearns for them. Here it is always summer. At times there isn't even a genuine spring. There isn't the joy of springtide, just as there isn't the despair and the death of winter."

HERE AND THERE

It did not take the colony long to discover that every mail brought us bundles of Yiddish newspapers from America. So they came and asked me to give them something to read. At first I wasn't at all pleased. The rôle of an Eretz Yisroel missionary in the cause of Yiddish was not to my taste. Besides, I didn't want to give old P. with the big blue spectacles the satisfaction of having his prophecy come true. This P., who was otherwise a very good friend of mine, had foretold a few weeks after my arrival in Rehoboth, that I would *smilingly* Yiddishize the entire settlement. And the very fact that I did not labor with might and main for the "Jargon", and was even friendly to Hebrew, made him consider me all the more dangerous.

But when I noticed the mountain of newspapers growing daily higher, and saw that there wasn't anything to wrap up in them, my resolution relaxed. Moreover, those who called for the papers were so persistent, that it would have required a heart of flint to refuse them. So I washed my hands of all responsibility. Let happen what might, and let the sin fall upon the heads of the offices that sent me the newspapers.

The papers were in great demand. They would be waited for with impatience and would pass from hand to hand. Some of the readers entreated me for mercy's sake not to let anybody else be the first to see them.

At first this gave me great pleasure. "There", I said to myself. "Let the Jews of Rehoboth learn what a fine literature we have developed in America." Later, when my "customers" began to inquire after certain issues, I began to grow suspicious, and a brief investigation revealed the fact that against my will, and unwittingly, I had helped to circulate in distant lands *The Lost Bridegroom* — "a Novel of Murder and Love, of New York life."

Together with the Jewish papers we received English journals—enough to supply a small library. Every one of our friends in America, wherever he might be, held it a sacred duty to send us one or more weekly or monthly journals. It is self-understood that every one selected the journal of his own preference, desiring us to enjoy it likewise.

The result was that we received magazines dealing with Sports, Medicine, Chess, and anything else you can imagine. That humor and wit are great favorites with my American friends was evidenced by the great number of comic journals they sent me.

A certain young American from New York never failed to send me "Detective Stories" every month. Another one was in the habit of sending me the "funny sheets" of all the New York papers.

Our American friend M. has received a guest from America—his brother from Pennsylvania, the owner of the house in which we live—in a way a "relative" of ours.

He visits us every day, and when he comes we go for a stroll in the newly planted orchard. Whenever we pass by a tree, he takes hold of the trunk and pats it with intense fondness: they are his representatives in Eretz Yisroel. If it weren't for his wife, who persists in waiting until the children have graduated from school, he would have been here with his family long ago.

He feels akin to us because every day we can look through our windows and see his Eretz Yisroel trees. He envies us this good fortune. In his remote Pennsylvania town, among the Slav coal-miners, his heart yearns for these trees, and he counts the days and weeks when his children will finish school.

This is the second time that he has come to inspect his property in Eretz Yisroel. When he returns from his journey and resumes his life in exile, he lives upon the pleasure of the days that he spent in Palestine, until a deep yearning once again dominates him and he returns to fill his spirit with Eretz Yisroel.

He has built up a great business in his home town. He is highly respected among the Gentile population, and there is no trace of anti-Semitism there. Yet daily he feels more and more an alien in the place.

He tells me that from his earliest childhood Eretz Yisroel has been the centre and the lodestar of all his thoughts. Later, when fate brought him to America, that feeling was strengthened. In his first years there he was a pedlar, and as he used to drive in his wagon from village to village, he would let go of the reins, let the horse amble on slowly through the mire, and give himself up to gloomy thoughts. He was a gypsy, without a home, without a land. His eye would fall upon the cakes of mud that had clung to the hoops of his wheels, and he would say to himself: "Here I sit with money in my pocket—my own money—and with my own goods in the wagon, and the wagon is mine, and the wheels are mine, but the bit of earth that has stuck to my wheel is not mine."

"And this tree which I did *not* plant, and whose planting I did not even witness, is my very own, and the soil is close to me and speaks to my heart."

This time he was accompanied to Palestine by one of the Gentile employes of his furniture business, who was very anxious to see "The Holy Land". He was a tall, muscular man, with straw-colored hair and large, clumsy hands, who had very little to say and was never in his life any farther from home than Pittsburgh. A glance at him was enough to show that he had lost all pleasure in the holiday, and yearned to be back in the furniture-store.

M. is a short, thin chap, and reaches only to his companion's vest-pocket. But the tall fellow holds on to M. like a sick child tugging at its mother's apron-strings. He is afraid to let him out of sight. Without him he feels lost.

His coming was evidently a great mistake. M. curses the day on which he thought of taking him along. Their trip to Jerusalem, whither the fellow-townsmen journeyed together and spent a few days, satisfied both, but the poor Pennsylvanian Dutchman spent a pitiable time in Rehoboth. In the first place, it doesn't look at all like "The Holy Land", and in the second, he is, in plain words, bored.

At the hotel, where M. has quartered him for the time he will remain in the colony, they don't understand a word of English, but the fellow, as was said, is not at all talkative. In fact, he would just as soon not speak at all. When it comes to meals, however, he gets the worst end of it.

When M. brought him for the first time to our house, he seemed to come to life anew. He became chatty, and took evident pleasure in the sound of his own voice, even as one takes pleasure in tasting a succulent dish that one has not been able to procure for a long time.

We offer him all sorts of English periodicals to read, but evidently reading had never been one of his weaknesses, so he thumbed them over out of politeness, and waited for us to turn our heads so that he might have a good yawn. My little daughter brought him a bundle of "funny sheets" that were months old, whereupon his nostrils distended, his eyes sparkled, and he threw himself upon the "Katzenjammer Kids" with as much joy as if he had just found a long lost brother.

. . . .

Last night I went with an acquaintance to hear Kinoth.

An elderly Jew sat near the almemar, upon the ground. He was swaying back and forth energetically, reciting "Lamentations". Around him stood a group of youngsters, listening to him out of curiosity. The

hoary-haired old men of the colony were seated upon
the earth, and, as it seemed, perfunctorily repeated
the words of the cantor with the ancient doleful
chant. Not a sound of weeping or groaning came from
anybody. The younger colonists stood in small groups
on the spacious veranda of the synagoague and chatted
about everything under the sun, or else silently watched
the moon as it came from Javneh and shone down
upon the gardens and orchards around the colony.

Perhaps there will come a time when the Ninth of
Ab will be a great holiday, and Jewish daughters will
come out to dance and frolic in the vineyards. In
the meantime this is the transitional period. The
Lamentations have lost the significance they had in
exile, and the new song is but now being created—the
gray twilight upon the eve of the future.

We went off to the Yemenites, and visited three different places of prayer. In each was felt the genuine, mournful spirit of *Tish'ah be-Ab*. The whole
assembly recited "Lamentations" in a doleful chant,
and many wept bitterly.

Outside, around the doors and the windows of the
little synagogue, squatted Yemenite women. One of
them was sobbing aloud. God alone knows whether
it was because of the destruction of the Temple, or
because her husband had forsaken her for a younger
wife.

On our way back we encountered a group of Yemenites walking silently and hastily by the olive groves.

The funeral of a child. One of them bore the tiny shrouded corpse in his arms, and the other carried boards, a spade, and other burial implements. They passed us, and hurried off in the direction of the cemetery. Behind them scurried their strangely elongated shadows.

VINTAGE

The kerosene boxes upon the steps of Padua's grocery are idle and forsaken. There is nobody to sit upon them and discuss politics, or criticize the village leaders, or pass the time jesting. The colony is now entirely given over to almonds. Everybody is taken up with almonds, and poor Padua, as he weighs a pound of rice, wonders when he'll ever be able to own a little garden or a vineyard, and be rid of his shop-keeping business.

After the almonds will come the grapes, and the labor and patience of an entire year will be rewarded with God's blessing. How many nights have the growers waked in the midst of a storm, trembling for the tender white blossoms. Then they would fear the hail or a violent downpour. Now all anxiety was at an end, and since everything thrived, this year, the settlement is gleefully astir, as if in preparation for a great holiday.

After the almonds were picked from the trees, they were brought in large sacks and spread out upon the ground.

On the next day three thousand Arabs, large and small, besieged the peaceful colony like locusts, and scattered in the yards beleaguering the doors of the colonists. They came to offer their services as almond shellers.

For the most part they were small children and women, starved-looking and half-naked, from villages near and far, to earn their five or ten *metalliks* per day, as the case might be, in addition to the opportunity to gorge themselves with almonds—a dainty that is never glimpsed in the Arab village.

About fifteen Arabs, grown-ups and tots, are seated in Khawaja Musa's yard, under the broad eucalyptus, around a heap of almonds, shelling them with their black, long-nailed fingers, or, more often, with their sharp white teeth. As soon as one of them has filled a kerosene tin, he brings it to the overseer. Whereupon a quarrel ensues as to measure: the overseer asserts that it isn't full enough, while the woman swears with the most sacred oaths that she packed and packed until there was no more room. After they have come to an agreement, the sheller pours the almonds into a heap near the house. This means five *metalliks*.

In the meantime there is somebody who keeps an eye upon the shellers, lest they eat more than they shell. Should one's eye be turned away for a moment, they stuff them into their cheeks as if they had been on a long fast. An Arab is never restrained by the danger of over-eating. Moreover, there is very seldom any opportunity to eat one's fill, not only of almonds, but even of dry "pitte".

I notice among the grimy, ugly Arab women a pale face with blonde hair. Her features were refined and aristocratic, and the whole impression not at all *fellahish*.

God knows when the blood of an *Ifranji* stole into the family genealogy. Perhaps at the time of the crusades?

Among the tiny Arab children sits old Abdallah, whose jaws quiver with age. He is a hundred and three years old, and can recall Ibrahim Pasha at the time he marched through Palestine. His old age is not a very happy one. His son, who is his support, beats him from time to time. The old man is seated near a sack of almonds, and is quarrelling with the ten-year-old Said over a shelled almond that the tiny fellow has stolen from under the aged man's withered hands. Both shout and curse each other as if they were of the same age.

I suggest to Abdallah that he let me photograph him.

"Tayyib, Khawaja". But he must get "baksheesh", or else he would not consider the proposition.

I offer him a *metallik*, to be paid in advance.

He shakes his head. It's worth two *metalliks*. He can't do it for less. I pay the two *metalliks* and tell him to get ready to be "snapped".

The youngsters roll on the ground with laughter as they see me focus the kodak, but Abdallah stands like a soldier, his hands at his side, and despite the fact that his one-hundred-and-three-year-old jaws move up and down, he is planted there as one transfixed.

Our neighbor, the lame blacksmith, was one of the first to gather in his almonds. "His almonds" meant no more or less than one sack, from the couple of trees that he had somewhere in his orchard. The sack was emptied amidst the broken carts and plowshares that lie around the smithy, and he and his wife, both of them proud and happy, sat a whole day shelling the nuts. They took their time, and evidently wished to prolong their pleasure as much as possible. Towards evening he brought us an earthen pot filled with shelled almonds: "Here, taste the *best* almonds in the colony."

For the children of the colony this season is a veritable holiday. My little daughter, in partnership with Khawaja Musa's little girl, shelled a whole boxful of almonds, for which they were promptly paid, in cash, five *metalliks*—two and a half a piece. Their joy was beyond description.

Before the shelled almonds had become dry, and while the sharp, sweet-sour odor of the heaped-up burs still tickled the nostrils, the vintage began. From earliest dawn the heavy clusters are cut in the vineyards and are placed in large, deep baskets. At night come caravans of camels and take the loaded baskets to the cellars of Rishon l'Zion, where the wine-presses labor day and night and cannot get through with their work.

Not all the grapes, however, are taken to Rishon l'Zion. Some are transported to the small *yekev* that the Aguddat ha-Koremim (Association of Vine-Growers) has in Rehoboth itself.

In the middle of the night, in the darkness of my room, I hear the slow, rhythmic strokes of the motor, and it seems that I can see the red blood of the grapes dripping into the vats. From afar comes the soft tinkling of the camels on the way to the wine-presses, and in one's dreams is spun the song of abundance.

We, too, so as not to be an exception, have in our orchard quite a few patches with vines. We have been counting upon the the vines since the first day we moved in. So we'll be supplied with grapes, and won't have to buy them, which is not an easy matter in the colony. The owners of the vineyards simply refuse to sell any grapes in the settlements. They really can't be blamed. There was one who sought such customers, but he will never do it again. The grapes were quickly snatched up, even before they were ripe. But since everybody purchased on trust— everybody buys on trust in the colony—and since it didn't look well to ask payment for a basketful of grapes, the colonist was almost ruined.

As I say, we had a little vineyard of our own. But thanks to Bennie and the jackals, we didn't taste a grape.

Bennie is a fellow of about eighteen, with a grimy face, who goes about in rags, in large torn shoes out of which stick his misshapen toes. No matter how often his family clothe him in new garments, the next day he hasn't a whole thread on his back. He chums with the small children of the colony, and is very often in our yard, hovering about the smithy. He helps the limping blacksmith hold the wagon when a wheel is to be put on, runs errands for his wife, and is quite a member of the family. Bennie is always hungry, and is exceedingly fond of almonds and apricots, when they are still as hard as stone. Sour grapes are the daintiest dish for him, and from the looks of things he found, in our orchard, the sourest in all Rehoboth.

The ripe grapes are eaten at night by the jackals. They steal right under the window, and select the ruddiest and juiciest. If only they committed their depredations silently it would not be so bad. But they have the ugly habit when they go foraging on alien property to utter wild howls, as if we owed them something for their trouble.

THE HURRICANE

The slender thread snapped, and the sword has fallen. The heavy storm that has hovered above the heads of the Western world has burst, and the crash speedily re-echoed in Palestine. From mouth to mouth leaped the bloody word: War.

Uncertain fears invaded the spirits of men. Events, like the misfortunes of Job, followed fast one upon another, and the cloud that sped from Europe spread and grew daily, hourly greater.

From Stamboul came orders for the reserve to mobilize. And all day long, tattered and barefoot Arab reservists tramped over the hot sands to Jaffa.

My little daughter was not well, and the doctor of the colony advised us to take her to the shore. I felt disinclined to leave Rehoboth, even for a short time. We had already come to feel at home in our new surroundings, and I used to say to my aquaintances that my soles were beginning to feel heavier—a sign that I was growing attached to the soil. But as it was impossible to bring the sea to Rehoboth, so, much against our will, we had to pack up and go to Tel-Aviv, for three or four weeks at least.

We reached Jaffa at about eleven A. M. I had a draft of the American Express Company on the Ottoman Bank. So we left the *khan* at once to collect the money.

We passed the city hall, and all at once found our-selves in the midst or a thousand-headed throng of Arabs. On the steps of the building stood a military officer delivering a patriotic speech. But the crowd was very calm. This tranquil behavior of conscripts surprised me greatly. I ascribed it to Mohammedan fatalism. But this impression was quickly dispelled by the remark of an acquaintance: "It is because they have not any 'fire-water' in them."

On my way to the Ottoman Bank, I stepped in to the Anglo-Palestine Bank, to greet my friend.

The bank was packed with people, and it was with great effort that I pushed my way toward his desk. He was surrounded on all sides by merchants, tourists, and depositors to whom he was for the tenth time repeating that the Anglo-Palestine Bank, like all the other banks in Palestine, had declared a moratorium, and that from that day forward the Bank would not pay out, even to the heaviest depositor, more than a hundred francs per week. This statement created a commotion, particularly among those who had to leave soon. There were some who only a day or two before had deposited large sums. The news struck them like a thunderbolt from a clear sky. On all sides were seen worried, despondent faces, and the excitement at the Bank rose from minute to minute. All the windows were besieged, and the employees wore themselves out and grew hoarse, answering the same questions over and over again.

Nor were comic contrasts lacking, as is usually the case in such circumstances.

An elderly Jew with a fine beard, parted in two strands, that tapered down to his chest, comes up to G., and demands his money. G. smiles in as friendly a manner as he can, and says: "A moratorium has been declared."

"Mo–ra–to–ry?" queries the man slowly, stroking his fine beard.

"Exactly."

"Well, as you say, then. And good-bye to you."

In a short while the same man is back again, this time all wrought up.

"Tell me, I pray, what sort of thing is this moratory of yours?"

When the swarm about G. has thinned somewhat, I take advantage of the opportunity to grasp his hand. I find him exhausted and all broken up. His eyes are moist.

"You see," he says to me, "I've been doing this from early morning. I haven't had a free moment. They won't believe me. And yet"—his sad eyes flare up with pride—"we are the only bank that is paying even a small amount. The other banks, with the exception of the Ottoman Bank, have stopped payments altogether."

I tell him that I have a draft on that Bank.

"Where is the draft?"

"I have it here."

"Cash it at once, and take whatever they give you. Later you won't get anything", he whispers into my ear.

Coming to Tel-Aviv I happened to fall in with a young Poale-Zionist from Canada, a sturdy fellow in working boots, with a tanned face. He tells me that he has been here for a couple of years and that he is highly content with Eretz Yisroel. His face beams with joy, and gives ample testimony to the fact that he certainly does not long for the flesh-pots of America. He is now working together with a co-operative group in the colony Petach Tikvah.

"Wouldn't you like to take a trip over our way and be the guest of the co-operative? They are a fine set —all of them—and we live in an orchard. And the room we have there makes your Montreal hotel look cheap by comparison. We'll give it over to you entirely, and the co-operative will sleep on the roof."

I grasped the opportunity. I had long desired to see the largest Jewish colony in Eretz Yisroel, which I had pictured to myself—and I don't know how such a conception ever came to me—as the ghetto of the new settlement. But I didn't have the tourist's reason for hurrying, so I had postponed my visit to Petach Tikvah, as well as many other trips through Judea and Galilee, from day to day until a proper opportunity should present itself. This chance, then, was most welcome. I arranged with the Canadian youth to have him reserve seats for us on the coach, and to meet us at three o'clock in the afternoon at the *khan*.

About two o'clock, together with ten other passengers, we were seated upon the *diligence* that runs between Tel-Aviv and Jaffa, on our way to the *khan*.

When we had reached about half-way to the city we encountered another coach driving toward us at full speed. The driver was whipping his horses mercilessly, and he, as well as the passengers, all pale and frightened, cried to us to turn about and ride back as quickly as possible to Tel-Aviv, if we valued or lives.

To our question "What is the matter?" he merely replied:

"An attack. Fighting....Shooting...."

And without a hint as to where the fighting was going on or who was being shot, he sent the coach flying on.

Our driver at once turned about, and a few frightened passengers jumped down from their seats and started running on foot to Tel-Aviv.

From afar we could make out, running in our direction from Jaffa, a horde of persons on foot, and among them wagons, filled with passengers.

At Tel-Aviv, in the meantime, the terror of a pogrom has descended. All doors and shutters were closed, and the young men dashed for their revolvers.

The commotion and the terror lasted for about half an hour, which seemed an eternity. Finally it transpired that the panic had arisen from the following event.

One of the Arab reservists got wild and began to cry: "Death to the infidels." An officer commanded him to shut up, whereupon the infuriated fellow drew his knife and rushed at the officer. At this the officer fired at him point blank, killing him instantly. The shot threw terror into the midst of the thousand-headed mob that filled the square before the "Saraye". There was a wild running and commotion, and the Jewish shop-keepers closed their places in fright, despite the pleading Arab citizens who urged them not to do so, lest the panic become worse.

The next day martial law was declared in Jaffa.

We did not go to Petach-Tikvah, to the intense disappointment of our Montreal Poale-Zionist. The declaration of the moratorium and the incident of the slain reservist, and, more than all else, the declaration of martial law, created an atmosphere of uneasiness and anxiety. So we decided to abandon our original plan and remain only a few more days in Tel-Aviv, and then return to Rehoboth.

We promised the Canadian that we would come some other time. That other time, much to my regret, never arrived.

About two o'clock in the morning we were aroused by shooting near our hotel. We bounded up from our beds, hastily donned a part of our clothes, and dashed out into the street. The shooting drew nearer and was accompanied by the outcries of a large multitude. At the same time the weird music of flutes could be heard. Near the Herzliah we found a gathering of half-dressed men and women, who had heard the shooting and the music with high-tensioned anxiety as it drew momentarily nearer and nearer. The wild outcries became clearer. In the moonlight the frightened faces looked ghastly. If anybody uttered a word, all would glance sternly at him and tell him to be silent.

It was the Arab reserves marching toward Haifah. "Suppose they storm into Tel-Aviv, which to the Arabs has always been a thorn in their side?"

The following day we journeyed back to Rehoboth. The conversation during the entire trip turned on pogroms.

Opposite me sits the colonist V., a tall fellow, a giant, with a fiery red beard. He is more frightened than anyone else.

He notices upon my countenance a trace of disdain and understands that I am measuring his iron-muscled arms with my eyes. He shakes his head: "You imagine that I am a coward? Then let me tell you what a pogrom means. I lived through the one at Kishinev. That is what drove me to Eretz Yisroel."

He tells his tale. And when he comes to his father-in-law, whom he found bathed in his own blood, with one eye dangling on his cheek, the voice of this powerful Jew sticks in his throat, and his fiery moustache makes strange grimaces.

In the meantime we reach the sands of Rishon l'Zion —high, long dunes of golden sand, smoothed by the last breeze, and above the sand, a deep blue sky. No grass, no verdure—just sand and sky, both luminous like two clear, unbroken, fundamental notes in some great, simple music.

TERROR

The burdensome consequences of the war in Europe were felt more and more in the colony, and the situation grew daily more oppressive and serious. For a whole year they had been waiting for the almonds, for which Egypt had always been a near and convenient market. Every year, at this time, the Egyptian buyers would arrive and fairly tear the goods out of the sellers' hands. On account of the financial crisis that occurred in Egypt upon the outbreak of the war, the buyers from that country could no longer be depended upon.

As if to tantalize the colonists, the almond crop this year was greater than ever. And there they lay now, in the huge sacks, becoming daily drier and paler, and at the same time losing in weight. And the faces of the colonists grew daily more wrinkled and gloomy.

There was a frightful scarcity of money, and not a place where to borrow. From the Anglo-Palestine Bank, which has always been ready to help in a pinch, not a farthing could be obtained. The small sum that the bank at first had been paying out weekly to its depositors was no longer paid in gold. All payments were now made in checks. The checks were made out for round figures: ten francs, twenty francs, and so on. And when you bought something and had to get change, the dealer refused to "lay the living upon the dead"— to take paper and give back metal. So that the checks declined in value with each passing day.

In Rehoboth as well as in Jerusalem and all the other Jewish colonies, all sorts of paper bills for small sums were circulating, issued by the Wa'ad (council) of the colony, by the Aguddat ha-Natto'im (Association of Planters) or by private individuals. They were accepted as currency among the Jewish population, and rarely was anyone audacious enough to refuse them. The trouble lay with the Arabs. They would have nothing to do with the new paper money, and demanded to be paid for their products in ringing coin.

The women of the colony came together and resolved that if they were really to give the Arabs their last *metalliks*, the Arabs must, at least, be prevented from profiteering on their products, as they had recently been doing.

It was decided that no Arab should any longer go about from house to house vending his products. They must all assemble upon the market-place, where the *shomerim* would see to it that the prices did not go above a fixed scale.

The boycott collapsed shamefully. The Arabs, learning of the new decree, ceased coming to the colony altogether. It was all that could be done to induce then to return at the old prices.

Only now it became evident how much the colony, which provides Glasgow and Odessa with oranges, itself depends upon the surrounding Arabian towns for the most necessary sustenance, such as vegetables, eggs, and so on.

Every other day we would be visited by blind Ibrahim and his small grandchild, who sold eggs. We were favorite customers of his, and our credit with him stood very high. Often a week or two would pass by before he would come to collect what we owed him. But now if, after he gropingly counts out the eggs, we say to him: "Ma fish il-yom masari" (There's no money to-day), he scrapes the eggs at once back into his basket, takes his grandchild and strides out without even saying: "Good day to you". Whatever little cash can be procured at all must be reserved for the Arabs.

All communication with the outside world has been completely severed. Only the mail arrives—and that but seldom. For the little news of the great war that filters into our settlement we are indebted to the daily *Ha-Herut* which is printed on the previous day in Jerusalem, and whose special telegrams are said to be reprinted from the *Ha-Zefirah*. The newspaper has not yet worked itself up to the point where it could subscribe to that daily, so it depends upon the favor of a friend of the editor, who receives it from Warsaw. As soon as the *Ha-Herut* arrives, it is snatched up, and with the present hunger for news it is meagre fare indeed.

Sugar, petroleum, and a hundred other necessities, begin to give out, and the price continues to rise. Everybody tries to supply himself with provisions. People buy as much as they can get and lay it in for later. Each seeks to get ahead of the other. Fear of famine fills everybody with terror.

As soon as night comes, the colony is submerged in pitch darkness. Hardly anybody can afford the costly luxury of burning a lamp. So people stand around in the dark, in groups, and talk about the war—eternally about the war.

The worst sufferers are those who lived from hand to mouth. The *po'alim* go about without jobs, despite the fact that the orchards are now in need of plenty of hands. There is no money with which to pay, so that no hands are hired. On the faces of some of the young fellows may be detected the signs of hunger.

To our neighbor came a girl of eighteen—an intelligent young woman, evidently of a good family— who asked for employment. She did not care what sort of work. Her face is yellow, and she is on the point of swooning. And it transpires that she has not eaten for several days.

Many of the colonists who are Ottoman subjects have been called to military service, among them the zoologist Ahroni. Those who have been summoned are given the choice of either serving or purchasing exemption at the cost of fifty Turkish Napoleons.

Neither among the Jewish population nor among the native Arabs is there the slightest desire to join the forces of the sultan, where the soldier must live amidst such evil and repulsive conditions, that even the half-brutalized, filthy Muslim fellah tries to get out of serving. The latter will often maim himself so as to evade the Turkish army.

However, it was evident that the government was not as anxious to have the men serve as it was to have them purchase exemption for the fifty Napoleons. To-day as much as ever the Turkish empire maintains in full force the good old "Code *Napoleon*".

Many of those who declared themselves willing to serve were sent to Gaza, but from that point they were ordered back home.

Fifty Napoleons is a little fortune in Palestine, even in the best of times. And at the present time it is a vast sum. To make matters worse, the government demands that sum in gold. The time allowed is short, so that friends and acquaintances have to scrape together their last coin to raise the ransom. The Yemenites with the little hoardings they have are now the wealthy magnates. One of the colonists borrowed forty Napoleons from his servant girl.

In addition to soldiers the government is demanding produce, sheep, and so on, from the colonies. If the colony hasn't the produce or sheep requisitioned, it must pay their value in gold. Whereupon once again the sum must be hunted high and low, and be ready for the appointed day.

Besides money the government demands wagons and horses for Suhra (compulsory work). In the middle of the night there is an alarm, and Turkish *hayyals* come and open up the barns, leading off the best horses to Jaffa. Days and days pass by, and when the owners are notified to come and take back the horses, the animals are found in such an exhausted state, so famished, that they are useless for any further work. As soon as they have been fed back to their proper condition, the soldiers come anew and take them off once more.

On account of the lack of wagons and horses the vintage has been crippled. "Reb" Yosef is afraid to venture forth from Rehoboth on his *diligence*, lest his span of horses be taken away from him, and when he does risk a journey he uses bony nags with just enough skin to hold the ribs together. And even then he is all a-shiver during the whole trip.

Many Arabian recruits were taken. Some hamlets were totally emptied of young men, being left with only gray-beards and women.

Because of the great number of recruits they had furnished, or perhaps because of political winds that had begun to blow from a certain direction, the Arabs began to feel important.

Inciting handbills were distributed among the natives in the villages. The behavior of the Arabs toward the Jews became constantly more insolent and ill-tempered, and there began to be heard such expressions as: "Soon the time will come when we can get even with the Yahud."

Old Madame E., who together with her husband went through the very earliest pioneer days in Rishon l'Zion and who in the good old days would single-handed engage in a fight with an Arab, says that an Arab threatened her:

"Wait, wait! 'Kurban bairam' will come and we'll slaughter you all like sheep."

For that matter the Arabs that come visiting the colony, with the natural envy that hungry indolence harbors toward industry and prosperity, have long since made a division of Rehoboth. Every one of them has mentally pointed out to himself the house of the Khawaja that he will take over as his own.

The air quivers with anxiety. People take fright at the least thing. A company of soldiers passed through the colony, whereupon the colony trembled for hours. It is rumored that the government wishes to instal Turkish *hayyals* in the colony, instead of the Jewish *shomerim*.

Our neighbor, the lame blacksmith, has come to us for a loan. He has a good pistol, and wants to buy a supply of cartridges so as to be ready.

I recall that a few weeks ago, while in my room, I suddenly heard firing. When I ran into the yard, I beheld this neighbor of mine shooting a cat. She had stolen into his coop, and was eating his little chicks, so he had sentenced her to die by shooting. The judgment, however, was far easier than the execution. For an hour later, when I went into the yard again, I found him still shooting at the same cat. He wasn't much of an expert in marksmanship. My desire for laughter disappeared, however, when I discovered that he owes his lameness to a pogrom in Russia.

My friends and neighbors advise me to leave.

"We have to stay. There is no help for it. But why should you go through unnecessary agony?"

I receive their advice as a bitter reproach.

After all I am not yet a citizen of Eretz Yisroel.

The aged pioneer H., one of the old-time *Biluists*,* now a hoary colonist, came from Hederah especially to see me. A mutual friend of ours had written him from America that he must by all means see me and ask whether I needed any money. And he came to fulfil his mission.

"And where will you get your money from now?"

"I'll borrow it for you," says the good old fellow, and the sun of Eretz Yisroel beams out of his youthful, black eyes.

I thank him for his kind intentions, and tell him that we'll manage to get along somehow or other, until funds arrive.

He feels rather slighted by my refusal.

We drink tea, and the old man, as fresh and lively as in his early *Bilu* years, tells me tales of to-day and yesterday. His countenance, passing quickly from melancholy to rejoicing, is a study in chiaro-oscuro. His strong faith struggles against hidden pangs. And as we bid each other good-buy, he lowers his voice, as if ashamed to speak his words:

"We wished to build a home for our children, and we haven't even reared one for ourselves."

*Name of an organization of students who in the eighties forsook home and career to emigrate to Palestine where they engaged in manual labor. The name *Bilu* is composed of the initials of the Hebrew words for "House of Jacob, come and let us go" (Isaiah 2.5).

A DELEGATION

Turkey is already enjoying the benefits of the war. First of all, a decree from Stamboul did away with foreign mail-service. There is no more Russian, French or Austrian postal service—there is only a Turkish one. In a way I am pleased with the new arrangement on account of the beautiful Turkish stamps. I also like the beautiful Ottoman law, according to which sending a letter to Jerusalem or Mecca costs but half as much as elsewhere. Even such a dry, practical organization as the post-office does not lose its reverence for the Holy Cities.

The stamps, like most Oriental things, are manufactured in London. And at first there was a scarcity of them. The abolition of foreign mail service came so suddenly, and the demand for Turkish stamps became so great, that there was no time to provide enough.

The government changes did not stop with the mail. Now, at a time when all the European nations were wooing the good graces of the Sublime Porte, has come the psychological moment to shake off the shame of generations—the capitulation system. The Ottoman empire declared itself of age and sole master in its own land. No consul could henceforth build up a government within a government. The foreigner, from this day forward, must trust in Turkish justice.

The news was received with great joy by the Arabs of Jaffa. They paraded through the streets, singing this song: "El-hamayah taht es-surmayah." (The capitulation is under the slipper).

We are living upon a volcano, which at any moment threatens to erupt. But even upon the edge of a volcano's crater, life quickly adjusts itself. Despite the panicky economic conditions of the colony, despite the insecure, ominous aspect of the political situation, little by little the people grew accustomed to them.

With characteristic energy the town council set about alleviating as far as possible the scarcity of money and the need among the inhabitants, and did its best to prevent the cessation of work in the orange-groves.

A communal store selling groceries and other necessary articles was opened. Every inhabitant received a certain amount of credit and the workmen, who are paid in scrip, could exchange it for merchandise.

At night the merry songs are heard again. The chief singers are a group of young chaps, students and artists, who have come for a tour through Eretz Yisroel and, because of the war, have been left stranded without funds to return. The community has given them the kindergarten as a lodging house, and the young people have instituted a communistic domestic régime. The women, especially the girls of the colony, have brought together the necessary paraphernalia, and have taught the communists housewifery, and more particularly the secrets of the culinary art.

In the group there are a poet, a cartoonist, an impressionistic painter, a reporter on a Yiddish newspaper, and a student of philology.

The division of labor among them is excellent. The impressionist is charged with scrubbing the floor, the poet's "mission" is to peel potatoes, the comic artist and the reporter see to the soiled clothes. The young linguist goes daily to market with a basket. Those who are not busy in the commissary department sew on buttons or perform similar duties.

The commune did its work so skilfully, that it had time left for the issuance of an illustrated journal of "art," literature, and humor — in two languages, Hebrew and Yiddish.

In the evening the young "housewives" would go out strolling with the daughters of Rehoboth, and their songs would banish all gloom. The population, especially the younger set, would forget all their troubles.

In the meantime the murder trial that had been going on between the Jews of Rehoboth and the Arabs of the village of Zarnuka came to an end. Both sides were acquitted. Young W., who had been in prison for a year, returned to the colony, to the intense joy of all, especially his father, half-farmer and half-butcher.

Those colonists, who dwelt in daily terror of being at any moment arrested, were for the first time in months able to appear upon the streets without fear.

The leaders then bethought themselves of the thanks due the old Sheikh Abu-Halib.

Abu-Halib lives far from Rehoboth—in the city of Hebron. But his name reaches to all corners of Judea. Everywhere people know Abu-Halib the peacemaker. It is a tradition in his family, and descends from father to son. Should a quarrel break out between one village and another, or between two neighboring tribes, behold Abu-Halib coming first to one side, then to the other. He strokes his long white beard, and speaks in a slow, deliberate manner. He tells what the prophet (Allah's blessing and peace upon him) says in the Sublime Book. He reproves and gives counsel, and his words fall like balm upon their hearts and like a cool breeze upon the inflamed spirits. They all listen to old Abu-Halib as to the prophet himself, and his words are worshipfully obeyed.

Abu-Halib is wealthy, and Allah has blessed him with fields and gardens, flocks of sheep, and countless camels. For his peace-making he asks no reward. He has a young son, and already the boy is following in his father's footsteps, and tries to make peace wherever he can.

At the time of the clash between the Jewish Shomerim and the Arabs of Zarnuka, when the colony trembled in fear of the vendetta-seeking relatives, messengers were sent after Sheikh Abu-Halib, entreating him to bring about peace and prevent unnecessary bloodshed. Whereupon the sheikh responded to the call, came from Hebron, and pleaded long and eloquently until the Zarnukians saw that it was more profitable for them to dwell in peace with their neighbors. A sheep was then slain, a feast was held in a vacant square in the centre of the colony, and both sides sat together, and swore friendship to each other.

The cursed trial, however, from which both the Rehobothans and the Zarnukians had sought with might and main to extricate themselves, still hung over their heads. Now that the trial was ended the community resolved to demonstrate their gratitude to the old sheikh by presenting him with a gift and an appropriate speech to go with it. For this purpose the communal assembly selected two messengers—Khawaja Musa and the old asthmatic G., one of the most energetic spirits in the colony, despite the fact that he is always very ill.

During the course of the trial G. would journey to Jerusalem every other week to see whomever he could and do whatever was necessary. He would usually be accompanied by Sh., a lanky, thin Jew with red hair, likewise a sick person.

In the colony they tell tales of how these invalid public personages used to nurse each other in the hotel at Jerusalem where they would stop.

At night, when G. would be seized with a fit of coughing, and would be gasping away for dear life, Sh. would bound up like a hero from his bed, and like a faithful nurse would tend his partner and bring him to. But no sooner would G.'s attack of choking cough pass, and he could breathe again, than Sh. would fall upon the bed and cry out:"Reb Shloyme, I'm a goner." Whereupon G. would set about to restore him.

As the healthier members of the community were among the defendants, there was no alternative but to send these dying representatives.

I desired very much to visit Hebron, the city that is linked with the oldest and sweetest childhood memories of the Jewish race, and with the earliest and most precious reminiscences of my own childhood, when my lame rebbi taught me the story of Abraham and Sarah and the Cave of Machpelah. So I took advantage of the favorable opportunity, and went along with the community's emissaries.

We were accompanied to the station of Ramleh by other Rehobothans. The clerk of the community, with spectacles and with a black, trimmed beard rode along, and kept sighing because, on account of the the European war, it was impossible to buy herring. Apart from his clerkship he enjoys another distinction: he is the father of the most beautiful girl in the colony. I see her every time I go for my mail. If it weren't for her amber-hued hair, I would compare her to Shulammith.

The other fellow was the one-eyed head of the watchmen in Rehoboth—a tall chap with red hair and a high fez. As he speaks he presses his thumb and his first two fingers together like a genuine Arab, smacks his lips, and reveals many signs of that Arabianization to which Khawaja Musa has often sighingly called my attention.

The road to Ramleh lies over deep sands. "Ramleh" is the Arabian word for sand. The cadaverous nags work with might and main before they manage to bring us into the vast olive-grove which is near Ramleh.

The trees are all of ancient origin. Many of the trunks are almost wholly rotten with age, but the branches are still productive. Olive-trees are long-lived, and those at Ramleh are doubtless hundreds of years old.

The local residents say that the trees date back from the time when the Second Temple was destroyed.

FROM THE MOUNT OF OLIVES

In the afternoon we left Ramleh for Jerusalem, reaching our destination toward evening and going directly to the hotel.

We were almost the only guests. It was long past the season for the tourists, and the war had driven foreign visitors from Jerusalem. The large salon and the dining-room, where year in and year out, at the price of ten francs per person, a "patriarchal" Passover feast is staged, were dark and dreary. The portrait of Moses Montefiore looked gloomily over to old Queen Victoria, who languished on the opposite wall. A portrait of the Spanish king—and God alone knows how he had ever managed to get there—glowered angrily at Herzl's picture.

The maitre-d'hotel, a tall Sephardi with a thick, black moustache and black, arrogant eyes, sat in a corner with his hands crossed, yearning for the tourists.

As we entered, we were shown to our room by a buxom, bare-legged maid in slippers. There was no excess of enthusiasm in the welcome accorded us. Jews from a colony.... Much business one might expect from them!

After our meal, Khawaja Musa and I went off to visit Dr. M. The inevitable squabble about Yiddish versus Hebrew ensued. This topic had already become so boresome to me that I was minded to pin a large placard to my lapel: "All discussions on the question of languages strictly forbidden." I was delighted when the talk shifted to the medical dictionary that M. is planning to write.

As the Hebrew University is now more than a possibility—I have already seen the site that has been purchased for that purpose—the preparation of a medical terminology will be urgent.

Together with Dr. M. we went to a meeting of the "Beth Lehem we-Teh", where daily bread and tea are distributed to thousands of people who have been left utterly destitute because of the war.

The speakers were almost unanimous in their protests against the methods employed by the representative of the German *Hilfsverein* to win back his influence among the people of Jerusalem. Since a large portion of the budget comes from the American Aid Fund, and the above-mentioned representative is the distributor of the fund, he has the poor practically in his power.

The workers, who are devoting themselves to the cause day in and day out with untiring energy, refuse to carry on their labors any further under his direction. They cannot forget the treacherous rôle he played when all Jerusalem and all Palestine fought as one man for their most precious and sacred possession— the Hebrew language—while he insisted on German as the official tongue for the schools.

The workers had independently assumed the burdensome task of collecting money and food for the hungry sufferers of Jerusalem, all in the spirit of self-help. They felt proud in the thought that the means of aiding the needy of Jerusalem came from Jerusalem itself. The consciousness of this fact strengthened their hands, and inspired their hearts. Now the American fund will kill this spirit of self-help and independence.

By the time we return to the hotel it is nearly midnight.

The streets are quiet and bathed in moonlight. Our voices ring out in the stillness with a strange echo. From the side-streets, from the yards, from the shimmering roofs, from the atmosphere, from all around, it seems, multitudes gaze down upon us, and listen to our conversation. If we cease speaking for a moment, the stillness becomes frightfully oppressive. The vast, unseen multitude is waiting.

For hundreds of years, for thousands—for God knows how many thousands of years—these multitudes have been waiting.

The next morning Khawaja Musa and I take a trip to the Mount of Olives.

We turn our glances in the direction of the mountains of Moab, which are discernible in the distance. Above them a white mist lazily hovers. On one of these mountains—Mt. Nebo—stood the great leader, and looked down upon the Promised Land, and thought of the people whom he loved more than his own life— the people he had fed and nourished with the blood of his own heart. There he stood and gazed mournfully and lovingly at the land from a distance. For the great Jehovah had said to him: "Get thee up into this mountain of Abarim, unto mount Nebo, which is in the land of Moab, that is over against Jericho; and behold the land of Canaan, which I give unto the children of Israel for a possession... For thou shalt see the land afar off; but thou shalt not go thither into the land which I give the children of Israel."

Whereupon the prophet bowed his head before the Lord's decree. He stood upon the summit of Mt. Nebo, and his eyes were drawn yonder toward the heritage of his people, and the mist upon his eyes was denser than the mist that now crawled over the blue hills of Moab.

Below, at a distance, the Dead Sea glitters in the morning light with the brilliance of freshly melted lead. And yonder is a tiny ribbon of the river Jordan, the small river Jordan, whose name is sacred among all peoples and in all lands, whose waters are transported to the remotst corners of the world as a consecration and a blessing at the cradle and a consolation and sacrament at the death-bed.

One's feet leave the solid earth. I am in the Bible as if in a fragrant field of tall grass. I wander through the verses, touch them with my fingers as one touches the green stalks in a meadow. The world of reality is far, far away.

We descend the hill on foot. We clamber through the Jewish cemetery. It seems as if the graves, and the stones that lie flat above them, will never end. But above the graves and above the tomb-stones dance myriads of sunbeams, and death lies warming itself in the sun.

We pass the Russian church. The gilded spires around the dome look like huge, golden organ pipes, ready to intone a hymn to the blue sky.

Deep down there is the valley of Jehoshaphat. That is where the great Day of Judgment will take place. All the graves in all the corners of the world will open, and of themselves the dead from every land and every age will arise and come to stand before the seat of judgment in that valley.

Across the valley is *Har ha-Bayit* (Hill of the Temple) and the "Dome of the Rock", or, as it is mistakenly called, the Mosque of Omar.

This is the location of the rock where the miraculous horse "El-Burak" brought the prophet of Allah, in the "Leylet el-Mi'raj" (the night of the Ascension), all the way from Mecca. And when Muhammed rose upon "El-Burak" into heaven, the rock wished to fly after him, but "Jibril" held him back. To this very day the mark of the angel's hand upon the rock is shown.

On the *Yom el-Kiyamah*, when the ram's horn shall blow, the black Ka'bah stone will come from Mecca on a pilgrimage to the rock upon the hill of the Temple. And God will sit upon the rock, and will judge the dead of all lands and of all ages that shall be gathered before him in the valley below.

Bright-gray Jerusalem, the Holy City, lies dreaming her great, immortal dreams in the splendor of the sun. Dreams of ancient, by-gone epochs and dreams of great days yet to come. Church towers and minaret spires stretch into the clear, blue sky. New buildings stand side by side with the old. A harmonious chant of all ages, of all nations, and of all gods.

Another member has joined the delegation that is to journey to present Sheikh Abu-Halib with the gift of the Rehobothans—the lawyer Mani, a short, corpulent Oriental Jew in a red fez, whose looks remind one very much of the Sultan Abdul Hamid.

Mani's family comes from Mesopotamia. About seventy years ago Mani's father came from there to Eretz Yisroel, and settled in Hebron. He was highly respected among both the Arabs and the Jews. To this very day pious Arabs come to his grave, to pray. Mani's brother is the *hakham bashi* of Hebron. He, the lawyer, lives in Jerusalem. He speaks Hebrew to us, but his mother-tongue is Arabic. He is a fountain-head of Arabian folk-lore and sayings.

He was the lawyer for the Rehobothans in the murder case. On account of his excellent Arabic he was selected to go along to Hebron. The Arabic spoken by Khawaja Musa and G. was rather inadequate for the flowery speech that must be delivered to Abu-Halib. Without the appropriate oration the gift would have lacked all flavor.

In the afternoon we got into a wagon, and drove off from Jerusalem to Hebron, or, as the Arabs call it: "Khalil er-Rahman"—the friend of God—Abraham. This is usually abbreviated to "El-Khalil".

The road meanders up hill and down. Long caravans of camels pass us by. These are army transports returning empty to Hebron. Mani keeps telling Arabian tales and discussing Arabian customs. As it is the time of "Kurban-Bairam", he tells us about that holiday.

"Kurban-Bairam" is the Turkish name for it, and means "The holiday of the sacrifice." The Arabs call it "El-'Id el-Kabir"—the great festival. On that day, every Muslim, no matter how poor, must slay a sheep. If he is not able to slay a whole sheep for himself, he "pools"together with others. Exactly thesame as atthe sacrifice of the Passover lamb of the ancient Israelites.

Mani points to the *Har ha-Bayit*, and , in the opposite direction, to the Mount of Olives.

The Muslims say that in the end of days a bridge will be stretched from one mountain to the other, as thin as a hair and as sharp as a sword. The just will cross this bridge in safety, riding upon the sheep that they slew upon the "Holiday of the Sacrifice". The wicked will fall into Gehenna. This is the "Siratu'l-Mustakim"—the right path, which is referred to in the first *surah* of the Koran.

We pass a gate bearing a Greek inscription. Through this gate one drives up to the "Mar Elias" church, which was constructed by a certain Metropolite by the name of Elias, or Elijah. Later the Metropolite was forgotten and the place was connected with the name of Elijah the prophet. According to an old legend, this is the place where Elijah the prophet rose to heaven in a chariot of flame.

The Mohammedan Arabs were not to be outdone. So they associated the place with "El-Khadr," who is the Elijah of the Muslims. He is called "El-Khadr," the green one, because wherever he stops to pray, the spot beneath this feet sprouts with verdure.

The fellahin of the vicinity tell the following tale:

A poor woman and her son dwelt not far from El-Khadr's gate. Once she beat her son so mercilessly that he left her and sat down near the gate, weeping bitterly. All at once El-Khadr appears to him and says: "The kings's daughter Helena has gone mad, and there is no cure for her. Go to her, for you shall make her well." So El-Khadr took him, and led him to the palace of the king, and when the boy had come thither, he bowed before the king and said: "O king, I have come to restore your daughter's health." The king rejoiced greatly, and said: "If you cure her, then I will give her to you for a wife."

So he went to the princess, and no sooner had he entered her room than she became instantly well.

When the king beheld this he could not believe his own eyes, so overjoyed was he. But he looked once again upon the youth, and was filled with regret at having promised to give the princess as wife to such a common person.

So he spoke to him as follows: "If you wish to marry my daughter, you must bring as gifts four mules laden with diamonds and precious stones."

The youth left in sadness, and despaired of ever getting the princess. All at once El-Khadr appeared to him and said: "Go back to the king and ask him for four mules with empty baskets. When they give you what you ask, go to the Wadi es-Sarar and load your baskets with pebbles, and bring them to the palace."

The youth did as he was told, and as he came to the palace and poured out the pebbles, it appeared that they were heaps of precious stones whose value was beyond computation.

So the king had to keep his word and give the youth his daughter for a wife.

We drive on until we come to a domed Mausoleum built in Arabian style. We stop.

"Mother Rachel's tomb."

I descend from the wagon, and enter the vaulted cave.

The walls are hung with silken curtains embroidered with gold letters and flowers. Wicks soaked in oil are burning in hanging lamps. In the midst of the cave, there is a large stone grave.

This is the anniversary day of Rachel's death, and the cave is full of worshippers. A young man in a prayer-shawl is praying before the altar with wild fervor. The others pray quietly, with heart-felt, exalted sincerity. The light from the oiled wicks blends with the cool shadows and with the murmurs of the worshippers in celestial melancholy.

A couple of women stand in a corner, and their lips move softly. One of them stoops down and raises a small, loose slab near the grave. She whispers a prayer into the opening, or perhaps she has placed her written supplication into it?

The young precentor recites the Eighteen Benedictions, and the assembly responds to every benediction with an "Amen" that seems to surge from the depths of their souls.

The wicks can be heard sucking up the oil, and a glimmer falls upon the stone, and upon the worshippers who feel a close intimacy with it.

At the entrance in the cave there is a well. A Jew scoops up some water in a little can and offers me a drink. The water is cool and refreshing. We leave the dark cave, walk into the clear, lambent air, and resume our journey over the winding road.

KIRIATH ARBA

It grows late, and we have still a long road to travel. Mani knows every bit of ground by heart. And every spot we pass has its own particular history. Here are the "Pools of Solomon", the reservoirs that the wise king had built, so that hilly Jerusalem might be provided with water from afar. Here is Bet Zur, where the Hasmoneans entrenched themselves against the Hellenic forces, fighting one against a hundred and ten against a thousand, for race and faith. Here is the grave of the gloomy moralist—the prophet Jonah. However desolate the vicinity, it is at any rate preferable to the inside of a whale. And here is the "Ramat El-Khalil", or the Elone-Mamre of the Bible. There stood Abraham's house, doors and gates wide ajar in every direction. And fine flour and cattle and sheep were ready for the hungry, dust-covered wayfarer.

Night descends. Over everything the moon has spread its diaphanous, magical veil.

Mani dozes off. The others are silent. The horses' hoofs clatter discordantly into the surrounding desert stillness. On either side of the road are fields and terraced hills, heaped up with white, porous stones which look like petrified mushrooms. My eyes are three-quarters closed. So the stones assume all sorts of fantastic forms. Now they are tomb-stones, now heaps of human corpses.

The night was already far advanced when our wagon stopped before the "Tamarisk of Abraham". The beautiful Hebrew name ("Eshel Avrohom") was the only beautiful thing about this hotel. It was a cold stone structure, as uncomfortable and as dreary as only an Arabian hotel can be—although the owners of this one happen to be Jews—grandsons of the famous Rabbi Shneor Zalmon Ladier. The Ashkenazi population of Hebron consists chiefly of Habadniks* and an appreciable number of the Ladier's relations.

A young boy with long ear-locks, a very active youngster with clever black eyes, hovers about us. He speaks Arabic better than Yiddish. His speech and gestures are "half Itzhok, half Ishmael", as the saintly Ladier would have said—or, as I put it, half hasidic and half Arabian.

The father is dead, and the hotel is run by the widow and her two sons, the lively youngster who serves us, and an older one, a youth of about seventeen, who walks about absorbed in thought and looks upon the hotel and the guests with intense scorn. If he is asked to do anything, he does it only perfunctorily. A bitter way of making a living!

The old Ladier is still in his veins.

We eat a wretched supper, and the delegates set about to fulfil their mission. A messenger is sent to tell

---

*A hasidic sect named after the initials of the kabbalistic words *Hokmah, Binah, De'ah* (Wisdom, Understanding, Knowledge).

old Abu-Halib that we are here and wish to visit him. The reply comes that he invites us to his home.

Our deputation is increased by two new members— two Hebron worthies of the Ladier family, tall young men with weak eyes, tanned faces, framed in narrow strips of black beards. They were those who had brought together the community of Rehoboth and Abu-Halib.

We walk through silent, slumbering streets. The Arabs go to sleep with the sun, and arise with the morning star. Not a light is to be seen in any house. We come to the gate of a court-yard, and a short avenue of trees leads us to a little garden behind a white-washed house. The garden is brightly illuminated by the moon. Rugs and cushions are spread upon the ground. The old sheikh comes out to welcome us. He is tall and straight as an old palm-tree, with a long white beard, a white turban and a loose, flowered smock fastened by a colored girdle. He greets each of us in leisurely fashion and with great ceremony.

"Tafaddal" (Be so kind).

We sit down in a circle. Coffee and cigarettes are served. All smoke in silence, and the smoke curls in blue spirals toward the moon and is lost in the trees. Then the real ceremony begins.

The learned G. dictates to Mani in Hebrew: "Abu-Halib is like unto Aaron the high priest, who was a lover of peace and a peacemaker. It was for peace that the Lord God created this world, and the guerdon that is destined to him who spreads peace is greater than that awarded for any other meritorious deed."

Then Mani turns toward old Abu-Halib, and begins to speak slowly, in florid fashion, counting every word, and all of us listen with rapt attention. And the learned asthmatic strokes his red beard, and the sheikh strokes his white beard, and after every sentence says: "Na'am" (yes).

When this speech has come to an end, G. brings forth the gift and presents it to the old sheikh:

"If the Jews of Rehoboth possessed Korah's treasures, they would not be able to repay you properly. They have therefore sent you a humble gift as a remembrance."

The old sheikh hesitates. His mild, deliberative voice possesses a world of peace and noble serenity:

He has always been a champion of peace. He wants no reward. It is all for the sake of Allah.

But G. insists, and Mani declaims another bit of fine Arabic oratory, this time his own composition, and we all sit there mute, while our eyes join in the entreaty.

"Tafaddal".

Whereupon old Abu-Halib accepts, and asks us to do him the honor of eating with him on the following day. We thank him for the great privilege, and decline. We must leave.

During the entire course of the conversation there sits beside Abu-Halib his father-in-law, likewise a venerable old man, but younger than he. This is the father of Abu-Halib's third and youngest wife.

We rise. Once more there is a ceremonious exchange of good wishes.

Blessings and compliments are uttered again and again, until we pass through the gate.

The next morning I arose early enough to behold, from the roof of "The Tamarisk of Abraham", the rising sun over the city of the Patriarchs.

About ten o'clock we went out on a sight-seeing tour of the city, which has a population of twenty thousand Arabs and about three hundred Jewish families. The Jewish population is growing and developing. Not long ago the Anglo-Palestine Bank opened a branch in Hebron.

We pass the Arab cemetery, which lies exposed in the very heart of the city, unprotected by any fence or wall—flat, gray graves, scattered in every direction without order. Out of every grave rise the two traditional pointed stones.

In the cemetery Arabs, men and women, stroll about or sit among the graves. The women are heavily veiled in black. They have come to the burial-ground in honor of "Kurban Bairam". The dead hover about their graves, and are not sundered from the living. The Arabian prophet, when he happened to pass a cemetery, would greet the corpses with a "Salam", as if they were living beings. It is a sacred custom to visit the dead on holidays just as one visits his living neighbors. And one feels quite at home with them.

The Arabs have a saying:

'Id al-Yahud bil-kudur,
'Id al-Nasara bil-zuhur,
'Id al-Arab bil-kubur.

The Jews celebrate their holidays with flesh-pots,
The Christians celebrate them with flowers,
The Arabs celebrate them with grave-visiting.

The Jews have, the Lord knows why, long enjoyed among the fellahin a reputation as gluttons. Whenever a Jew enters an Arab village, the children sing these mocking verses:

Ya Yahud, bikh, bikh,
Hut ras fil-tabikh.

"Oh Jew, oh Jew,
"Stick your head in the stew".

We enter the Jewish ghetto which consists of dark, filthy stone arches and alleys, and reach the residence of Mani's brother, the *hakham bashi* of Hebron.

The old man, a genial patriarch in his seventies, accords us a very hearty welcome. We sit down upon the balcony, and the *hakham-bashi's* wife serves us "shai" (tea). This is especially for us, as the usual beverage is coffee.

The wife of the *hakham-bashi* is some thirty years younger than her husband. She is Russian, and originally journeyed from Russia to Buenos Aires. From that city she came to a sister of hers in Rishon l'Zion. A match-maker brought her together with the widower. They are evidently very happy.

From where we sit we can descry the Arab cemetery which is at some distance. Around one of the graves a group of dervishes is performing a "zikr", dancing in an ecstatic circle. The dance begins slowly, step by step, and grows faster and faster. Mani tells us that they often dance until they end with a convulsive gasp and their mouths begin to gush blood. The dance we witnessed was much more restrained. I should say that it was not much wilder than the antics of an ecstatic Hasid at his prayers.

The *hakham-bashi* was preparing to visit the Mufti, the Kadi, and Kaimakam of Hebron, and offer them holiday greetings, as was his custom. In honor of this occasion he attired himself in his official vestments —a silver-embroidered turban and a silver collar upon his mantle. These garments—he tells us—are the same as those worn by the Muslim clergy, with the difference that the Arab decorations are of gold, while the *hakhams* must wear silver.

We leave the *hakham-bashi's* house, and go to see the Cave of Machpelah. Once again we pass through the ghetto. Mani points out the breach in the gate to the ghetto, and relates:

"Many years ago there ruled over Hebron a great Arabian Pasha who oppressed the Jews. Once he imposed upon the Jews of Hebron a tribute of fifty thousand dinars. Unless it were paid, he would have them all wiped out. The community was frightfully poor. There was no hope of getting together even a tenth of the sum. They proclaimed a fast, and besought heaven day and night. Meanwhile the appointed day was drawing nearer and nearer. Now the final night had come. The next morning the term expired, and the Pasha would slay every Jew. All at once, in the dead of the night, someone raps at the gate. The watchman refuses to open it. The stranger knocks so powerfully that he makes a hole in the thick wood of the gate. A hand appears which delivers to the guard something tied up in a kerchief, and a voice speaks from the other side of the gate. "Give this to the Pasha." And at once the hand disappeared.

The next day the leaders of the community go to the Pasha and give him the bundle. The Pasha opens it, turns pale, and begins to tremble like a leaf. Then he says to the community leaders: 'Know ye that last night I was visited by Father Abraham, and he demanded of me the jewels of my favorite wife. So I gave them to him, and here are the jewels in the kerchief.'

Whereupon the Pasha craved forgiveness of the elders, and ever since that time has been friendly to the Jews of Hebron."

We reach the Cave of Machpelah over which is built a lofty Jami'. On account of "Kurban Bairam" a large crowd of Arabs is entering it.

No steps of an unbeliever may profane this mosque.

A certain stone is pointed out to us, and we are told that Isaac lies underneath. We are shown the spot where Esau's head is buried. The body lies elsewhere. For this the deaf Hushim is to blame, and it came about in this manner:

When Jacob died, and his sons and grandsons brought him from Egypt to the Cave of Machpelah, Esau came with his sons, saying that the place belonged to him, and that the place assigned to Jacob had already been occupied by Leah. A quarrel ensued, whereupon Naphtali, whose legs were as fleet as an antelope's, was despatched to get the bill of sale, which showed black on white that the whole Cave of Machpelah was the exclusive property of Jacob. The mess of pottage had paid for everything.

Hushim, the deaf son of Dan, witnessed the wrangling, but as he could not hear a word of the arguments, he could not understand why the burial of his grandfather was delayed. So he seized a shovel, and, without so much as a "by your leave", he struck off Esau's head. Esau's sons became frightened, and seizing the body of their father escaped with it. The head, however, remained, and it was buried together with Abraham, Isaac, and Jacob.

On our way back Mani points to a mound under which lie buried the witnesses who were present when Abraham bought the Cave of Machpelah from Ephron the Hittite. Without these witnesses, God knows whether we should ever have had a Cave of Machpelah.

When Abraham wished to buy from Ephron a place in which to bury Sarah, the shrewd Hittite refused to sell him more than the area of an ox-hide. So Abraham said: "Good, I'll give you four hundred shekels for the space of an ox-hide." He called over Aner, Eshcol, and Mamre, and asked them to witness the bargain. Then Abraham went off, took the hide of an ox, cut it into narrow strips, and with them measured off the whole field of the cave. Ephron at first tried to deny the sale point blank, but Abraham brought his witnesses.

Whereupon Ephron flew into a murderous rage, and slew the three witnesses. This availed him nothing, however, for even after they had been buried and covered with earth, the witness kept crying from beneath the sod: "We are witnesses that Abraham bought the land."

AN UPHEAVAL

About one o'clock in the afternoon we left Hebron.

The surroundings of old Kiriath Arba (the city of the giant Arba) are planted with fertile vineyards. Hebron grapes enjoy the reputation of being the best in all Eretz Yisroel.

On our way to Sheikh Abu-Halib we happened to pass the river or valley of Eshcol, the place which, the Biblical verse tells us, the scouts reached, and cut down a branch and a cluster of grapes and bore it upon a pole. So that place was named "The valley of Eshcol", because of the Eshcol (cluster of grapes) "which the children of Israel cut down from thence."

The scouts brought the huge cluster of grapes, and said to the children of Israel: "A precious land. It flows with milk and honey; but—the people that dwell therein are too strong for us. We are not a match for them."

But Caleb, son of Jephunneh, arose and said: "Let us go and take it for our own...... For we will conquer them."

So Hebron was given to Caleb, "and he drove the three giants forth from that place," and he had no fear of the Hittites and the Jebusites. And huge, juicy grapes fell to his share.

We entered Jerusalem toward Friday evening. Our intention was to remain in Jerusalem over Saturday and to leave on Sunday for home. But an unforeseen upheaval forced us to leave before we meant to, and we were compelled to violate the Sabbath publicly by riding on the sacred day of rest in a wagon, through the streets of the Holy City.

We were eating our breakfast Saturday morning, when of a sudden the proprietor of the hotel came rushing in, pale and breathless, with the news that the Russian consulate had just hoisted a green flag, signifying that Turkey had declared war upon Russia, and that Russian subjects had been transferred to the protection of the Italian consul.

The news spread like wild-fire, and caused an indescribable commotion in the city. Since the majority of the Jewish residents of Jerusalem were Russian subjects, all were seized with panicky terror. What would Turkey do with the foreign subjects? They knew what Germany had done, and they had made their own deductions.

Khawaja Musa wished to go over to the Russian consul. I accompanied him. A tiny green flag flapped on high. And that little strip of green cloth was the symbol of a great misfortune.

Inside the consulate all was tumult and consternation. Chests and valises were being packed with documents and hastily sent off, evidently to the Italian consulate.

The consul himself and his Jewish aide were chalk-white, dashing hither and thither in confusion.

Khawaja Musa asked whether he should remain in Jerusalem. Would not all communication between Jerusalem and the outlying districts be cut off, as rumor had it? The advice he received was: Be off, be off, as soon as possible.

The air was filled with terror.

I went in to see the American consul, Dr. Glazebrook, and found him near his gate on horse-back, calmly preparing for a ride, with his wife and his "kavas".

I asked him whether he knew anything about Turkey's declaration of war. He replied: "No". I told him the news.

This does not affect Americans. However, he advises me to go back home to Rehoboth. We decide to leave at once. So G. sends for a rabbinic decision upon the question of journeying on the Sabbath, and receives the reply that under such circumstances it is permissible. But he is in despair. My heart goes out to him. For him, in his declining years, to violate the Sabbath before the public gaze in Jerusalem!

The driver knows how to profit by our hurry: he asks twice the regular rates. We take our seats in the wagon, and urge the driver on.

We are impatient to leave Jerusalem as quickly as may be. Together with us comes Dr. Rupin of the Palestine Bureau. We place old G. in the middle, trying to conceal him as well as possible. He turns up his

collar and lowers his head. If he could only hide under
the driver's box altogether!

The wagon rattles mockingly over the hard stones,
and taunts the Sabbath quiet with spiteful clamor.
Jews pause to look at the wagon and its passengers.

"What has happened?"

Nobody, not even the most spiteful apostate,
would go joy-riding in Jerusalem on the Sabbath. So
the people know that a misfortune has occurred.

An elderly Jew recognizes G., and opens his eyes wide
with stupefaction, as if the world itself had come to an
end.

We ride along, and our hearts are heavy. What will
become of the settlement now? Will the bloody deluge
carry off in its flood all that was planted and built at
the cost of so much sacrifice? What will the Arabs do?
Will they not take advantage of the hostility
against the Russians to wreak their fury upon the
Jewish colonists, who are almost all Russian subjects?

After a couple of hours of continuous riding, we stop
at Bab el-Wadi (The Gate of the Valley), an Arab village surrounded on all sides by hills.

The driver waters his horses, and we sit down upon
tiny benches near a coffee-house, ordering coffee for
the entire company.

The day is beautiful and the sunlight is soft and
caressing. The sky is blue and peaceful and the hills
round about look down upon us with unruffled serenity
and security. Something of that peacefulness filters

into our spirits, and through the gathering clouds we behold a light.

G. begins to feel remorse at having been persuaded to violate the Sabbath. Where is the danger?

As one gazed upon the restful and clear, assuring sky, it was hard to believe that elsewhere there were unrest and war and universal upheaval.

We reached Ramleh towards evening. There we bade adieu to Dr. Rupin. He rode off to Tel-Aviv by the wagon, and we remained waiting until the vehicle for which we telegraphed from Jerusalem would arrive for us from Rehoboth. It was late at night when it arrived.

At the limits of the colony the mounted Shomerim came out to meet us. Despite the heavy apprehensions that weighed upon our minds, our hearts bounded with happiness at the sight of *our* Shomerim, and at the thought that we had reached *home*, Rehoboth.

AFTER THE DROUGHT

The trees stretched languidly toward the sky. The breasts of mother Earth, which they had sucked for six months, were dry, not a drop had been left. Every leaf and branch was a mute, despairing prayer for rain. Black patches began to chase each other across the sky and then grew into a vast expanse of darkness. Out of the darkness issued a frightful rumble—a message that the gates of mercy had opened and that the prayer had been granted. Then for a whole day the colony was drenched in a heavy downpour, and with burning thirst the gardens drank in the first gifts of the wet season.

The next day the sky was bluer and more beautiful than ever. The trees eagerly sipped the drops that had not yet evaporated. Their thirst had been quenched, they were refreshed. Now they will wait for more. It will come a-plenty for days and days.

Days passed, a week, and about the synagogue the grass had become green again. Flowers began to peep forth. Spring was in the air. The first rains every year in Eretz Yisroel are a holiday for people and trees alike. This year, however, there is a damper upon the festive mood.

The fright and uncertainty that had fallen upon the Jewish population on the outbreak of the European war had subsided. Life had resumed, more or less, its normal course, and people began to breathe more freely.

Now, however, with the entrance of Turkey into the world war, panic broke out anew—darker and more threatening than before. Nor is the fright baseless. There are reasons in abundance to fill even the most determined with anxiety and trembling. The attitude of the government toward Jews becomes daily more hostile. At every opportunity the officials plainly show that they regard with suspicion the inhabitants of Tel-Aviv, the colonists, and especially the institutions of the new settlement.

The Anglo-Palestine Bank has been closed, and the cheques which it issued have been confiscated.

The commandant of Jaffa has sent an order that a certain number of rifles be delivered to him. He knows that there is a quantity of fire-arms in the colony, and wants them brought to him. When E., one of the respected leaders of the community, came to him, the commandant showered upon him the vilest curses.

"Do you think, you dog, that because your son is an officer in the Ottoman army I will have any regard for you? The whole bunch of you will rot in prison."

To the feeling of terror was added that of deep wrong and humilation.

Letters written in Hebrew are not accepted at the post-office. English and French, though they are languages of the enemy, are permissible, but not Hebrew.

The decree is a frightful blow to the Hebrew population, the greater part of which cannot correspond in any other tongue. Their hands are bound, their mouths sealed, and communication with the outside world is rendered impossible.

I strolled with S. far beyond the limits of Rehoboth. All at once we hear the throbbing of a motor. We imagine that the pounding of the wine-presses has been wafted from Rishon l'Zion to us, upon the slumbering air. Selim, who is working in a field near-by, hears more clearly than we, with those Arab ears of his.

"Tayyar, Tayyar."

We gaze up to the blue sky, and behold an aeroplane circling as gracefully as a proud bird of prey, now up, now down.

The first visit of the English.

Selim says: "We'll get even with the English soon enough, *inshallah*. Our soldiers will soon close up the Suez Canal. If each fellow takes one sack of sand it'll be enough to stuff up the whole canal."

Among the Arab population rumors have been spread that the sultan will very soon declare a *Jihad*. Whereupon the "sanjak sharif" — the green flag—will be unwrapped from the forty sheets in which it is now rolled up at Stamboul, and when it is spread out all the Muslims from the oldest to the youngest will march forth to battle and will not rest until they exterminate the enemies of Allah.

That which lay all this time like a nightmare upon everybody's mind, and which was bound to happen sooner or later, finally came to pass. An order came for every subject of any of the enemy nations to leave the land. But the Ottoman empire was merciful and permitted Ottomanization—one might become a Turkish subject and thus be saved from the decree. Whereupon the people began to Ottomanize themselves right and left. Naturally not without some trepidation, especially the younger element, who might expect to be called to arms at once for service with the Turkish troops. To make matters worse, it cost about two Napoleons to become a Turk by law, and not everybody had that amount.

According to the law, adult daughters became Turkish subjects on the Ottomanization of their fathers. Many girls whose families were elsewhere had themselves "adopted" to avoid the payment of the two lires which they could not raise. Thus the old childless beadle found himself one morning possessed of two handsome, grown-up daughters.

The newly naturalized Turks wear a red tarbush so as to inform the world that they are Ottoman subjects. This has altogether changed their appearance. Some of them look rather well in their new outfit, while others look absurd and pitiful. When you see Mayshe the asthmatic carpenter panting along in a high red fez, you must force yourself to think of death, in order not to burst into guffaws.

The little school children play at war. One is a Russian, the other a Turk. They beat the Russian mercilessly. The children are frightfully patriotic.

The pious old Jews of the colony say that this is the war of Gog and Magog, and that the redemption of the Jews is near. A devout old man, who spends his days in pious studies, arose in the middle of the night, awakend his household, and ordered many lights to be lighted, while he took up a position near the window, pale, dishevelled, with eyes aflame, and hands trembling, staring into the dense darkness.   And his old lips repeated: "He will be here at any moment. He is on his way. He is coming to us. Let us give him a hearty welcome."

And thus he stood all night long, not permitting any of his household to go to sleep. And the lights burned, and he watched for the Messiah until break of day.

DARK DAYS

One day the news arrived from Jaffa that all foreigners who had not become Turkish subjects must come to be entered in the "seraye", not later than the following day. Otherwise they would be interned somewhere in a remote spot in the interior of the country. This meant that all foreigners, without distinction, even American citizens, must answer the call. On the morning of the next day half the colony, including myself and other Americans, set out on the road to Jaffa. Some went by coach or by wagon, some on donkeys. But the majority went on foot. In the multitude were men and women, old folk and youths. The eighty-year-old cobbler, a shrivelled old fellow, walked beside the tall, stout midwife, and seemed even smaller and thinner by contrast.

This midwife was more afraid than anybody else of the Turkish government. A few days previous—as she tells us with a serious countenance—she dreamt that soldiers came and took her off by force to the army. She awoke affrighted, and ever since then the terror had entered her very marrow. Turkey was apt to do anything.

Gradually the sun grew warmer, and its rays struck mercilessly upon the heads of the pedestrians. The crowd was exhausted, and was walking on its last strength. Contrary to the general custom when people travel together in Eretz Yisroel, there was neither con-

versation nor laughter. The multitude proceeded mutely. Silently they dragged their feet along through
the sand, and wiped the perspiration from their faces.
The crowd kept close together during the whole time;
the wagons purposely rode along slowly, so as not to
leave the pedestrians behind. From a distance it looked
like a great funeral procession.

Our plan was to proceed at once to the American
vice-consul and find out what to do. But as the "seraye" was not far from the "khan" at which the coach
arrives, we went there together with the other Rehobothans.

There was pandemonium in the "seraye", and the
throng was dense enough to stifle anybody. Hundreds
of persons were pressing about the closed doors behind
which mysteriously sat the officials who entered the
names of the foreigners. Everybody tried to be the
first to get in. But the officials were not in the slightest
hurry. Between one opening of the door and the other
a long interval would pass, and only two or three were
admitted at a time. One needn't have been an expert
time-keeper to compute that not only would a day be
insufficient to enter all the names, but even a week.
Through the turmoil an Arab waiter of a near-by café
comes elbowing his way with a tray of thimblefuls of
coffee for the hard-worked registrars.

In the meantime new reports kept arriving. One
minute it would be that everybody might return to his

home in peace. A special committee would be sent to each colony. The next moment it would be that the inhabitants of the colonies in the vicinity of Ramleh must go there. The crowd did not know whom to believe, and there was nobody to give any reliable information. After strenuous efforts we managed to extricate ourselves from the crowd in the "seraye", and went off to Hotel Hardeg, the residence of the protector of Uncle Sam's citizens.

In the hotel office we found a score of American citizens, all of them children of Israel, who had surrounded the vice-consul, and were hurling at him an endless repetition of the same question: Should they or should they not register?

In addition to the American citizens there were a few English subjects, who since the declaration of war by Turkey had come under the protection of the American vice-consul, and felt in duty bound to bother him with all sorts of queries.

To tell the truth, the vice-consul had never set eyes upon "the land of the free." The office had come to him by inheritance from his father-in-law, together with the hotel and the father-in-law's name, Hardeg, which he had assumed. He was really a German by birth and breeding, born in Germany, brought up in Palestine, and devoutly pious. All the rooms in his hotel were named after the prophets. One was called Haggai, the other Malachi, a third Habakkuk. When the prophets had run out, and there were a few rooms left, he named them after the archangels: Raphael, Michael, Gabriel.

On account of the war he now found himself in the anomalous position of a German who, as American consul, must protect English subjects.

So there he stood now with a drawn face, lost and scared, glancing now at his besiegers and now at a side door, through which he evinced a great desire to make his escape. He was not at all prepared for such an emergency.

The distinction of being the one to cut the Gordian knot fell to me. I was struck by the "phenomenal" idea of suggesting that the consul's *kavas* should be sent to the "seraye", to find out for certain whether Americans were exempt from registration or not. In the meantime, let the crowd disperse for a couple of hours, thus giving the *kavas* time to fulfil his mission and us— to snatch a bite. The pious, quiet Hardeg seemed to have been born anew. The great idea was soon transformed from thought into action, and before we were aware of it, the protector of the "stars and stripes" had disappeared through the door upon which he had all this time been casting an eager eye.

We returned to our former hotel in Tel-Aviv. It was difficult to recognize the beautiful suburb. Everywhere was an atmosphere of depression and gloom. The lively, cheerful bustle upon the thoroughfares had ceased. Only at rare intervals would a cab pass by. People went about with worried faces, bowed heads, engrossed in their own sad thoughts.

The erection of buildings had come to a standstill. Those that had been begun some time previous were abandoned in the midst of the work, and this state of incompletion bore mute testimony to the ruin that the frightful war had brought to Jewish hopes.

The table of the restaurant, despite the fact that it was lunch hour, was three-quarters unoccupied. There were few now who could afford the luxury of three *bishliks* (about thirty cents) for a meal.

The usual merry table-talk was absent. It was as if each feared to look into the other's eyes. So everybody ate in silence, with eyes fixed upon the plate.

In the afternoon, when we returned to the vice-consul, we found waiting for us the reassuring news that Americans and citizens of all the other neutral nations were exempt from the decree.

At night we drove back to Rehoboth.

Gray, heavy days crawl one after the other. I had arrived in Eretz Yisroel at a beautiful, richly-dowered period. Everthing had been a symphony of light—the music of the vast future. Now all had turned black again, a-quiver with uncertainty. My heart is again assailed by doubts. I can hear them gnawing. Everybody around me is so dejected, so embittered, as if they regretted the whole affair.

The conversation turns mostly upon the high cost of provisions—the prices of wheat and flour, of petroleum and sugar. People tell each other where one may purchase a box of matches cheap.

In the centre of the colony stood a row of tall eucalypti, which lent a touch of beauty to the market-place. The owner had them chopped down, for the sake of the few *bishliks* she received for the lumber. I pass by the spot, behold the white, open wounds of the trees that have been cut down, and I am seized with anger. A stifling pain takes possession of me and gives me no rest. I begin to look for faults, and hate myself for doing so.

It occurs to me that many of the persons I see in Eretz Yisroel are there simply because they have no choice in the matter. Since they are either too old or too poor to return to Europe, they dream that through some miracle or other Europe will come to them. They would welcome that Europe, even if she were to restrict the freedom of Jewish national development. Not being able go to the flesh-pots, they secretly hope that the flesh-pots will come to them. And of a sudden I ask myself: Why has not Eretz Yisroel fructified us spiritually? Where is the song, the work of art, which was created in Eretz Yisroel? But I know that it is the war which is responsible for all this ugly questioning.

There is nothing to live on. So I live on the beautiful sunsets which have become a hundredfold more beautiful since the rain set in.

With the approach of evening the sun begins to play hour after hour like a long oratorio, pouring out one flood of color after another, each more glorious than the preceding. Never did I realize how unending was the profusion of hues, as I realize it now, after having witnessed the glories of the Eretz Yisroel sunset in the month of Heshwan.

The doubting questions have disappeared, and once again I hear—this time in soft, almost inaudible tones—the great, beautiful song of the future, the hymn of joy to the re-built Eretz Yisroel.

I return from my walk, and vow again that I will not leave Eretz Yisroel.

A LETTER

Dear...........

The postal service is now totally demoralized, and I mail this letter trusting to God's tender mercies. When it arrives (if, indeed, it ever does arrive), I may no longer be able to behold through the window, as now, my neighbor's tall, green eucalyptus, the loftiest in all the colony; and my eyes will no more repose upon the green, grassy hill that gazes down upon the synagogue and the cheery, white-washed school-house; and my lungs will no more inhale the fresh, invigorating air of Eretz Yisroel's autumn. All these things will have become memories, and at the thought of them the heart will grow heavy.

I am ashamed and anguished. Anxiety and shame flutter like dark bats in the midst of bright daylight, and every moment they strike against another nook of my soul.

I am ashamed.

The tormenting ghouls, whom I had shaken off with my first step upon the "gumruk" of the port of Jaffa, are waiting there now for me. As soon as the brown-complexioned "baharieh" will thrust the rowboat off from the landing, those evil spirits will spring forth from the rocks, and will gnash their teeth and begin to torture me, even as they have done many a year.

I had thought that the purgatorial period was all over for me. I had gone through the ordeal so happily, and had said to myself: "Now you may feel secure; the ground is firm beneath you, and not all the winds that blow will be able to uproot you." And, like one who has just been rescued from a shipwreck, I looked back at the uncertainty which I had left behind, and offered up prayers of thanks.

It began, as it does for everybody who comes here, with a holiday mood, an intoxication. Sunshine, sky, flowers, sea—all of this intoxicated one like old wine. The vessel was not large enough to contain all this wealth, the hands could not gather in fast enough all those treasures. Born anew, with limbs as light as wings and thoughts so unclouded and serene.

Then followed—perforce—a reaction, a personal accounting. This did not cross the lips, nor was it quite clear, and it feared to call itself by name. Whereupon all of you on the other side joined in, and pointed at me with your fingers: narrowness, impoverishment.

So I conjured up my first enthusiasm anew, and therewith shattered your weapons. I had to vindicate myself. But I had no arms against myself.

Those were hard days. I could find support nowhere. The old agonies had been increased by another—self-mockery.

Those were painful days, but they were followed by recovery—the genuine love for the land. Eretz Yisroel kept growing and growing, widening to the most distant horizons, and became as vast as my entire world. To be more precise, Eretz Yisroel had become so vast that all my worlds entered into it, and were able to expand and expand. And I no longer said: "It is worth the price I am paying." For it was no longer an exchange. It was not a sacrifice. I became richer and fuller, and it was now my turn to pity you: *You* were the poor ones. All your lives were spent in making syntheses, and you were forever patching and mending and piecing together. The Lord had blessed you with clever heads, and you are masters in all sorts of sophistic ingenuities. So that you had somehow or other patched together a thing that looked whole.

But the garment rips here and there, the stitches are botched. And however skilfully you may do the work, it is still inadequate. So that you must keep turning about this way and that to hide the ripped seams.

And that turning is so unnatural, so ugly, for everything that is unnatural is ugly.

Am I to return where this patching and argumentation are going on? My pride has grown to such gigantic proportions during the last year. I must have acquired it from the lofty eucalyptus. I have become so exacting. I demand the fullest measure of racial assertiveness, and will not relinquish an iota. And to pause for arguments, for the making of syntheses, for supporting with logical acumen that which sings within me like a mighty hymn and burgeons and grows about me in every nook is, in my eyes, beggarly pettiness, beneath contempt.

And now all this would cease, and there would return the ancient coil of contradictions, the maze of doubt and faith, of real grief and assumed joy, of unspoken despair and bolstered-up courage.

Now we shall have to live again upon crumbs. I would be thrust away from the richly laden table and have to learn again the art of being content with little.

I still cherish in my heart the hope that this will not happen. And if I leave my sunny Rehoboth, it will be only for a while—on a visit to Egypt. There we shall wait for the storm to subside. There I shall hide me in some remote spot, burrow into it and dream of Eretz Yisroel.

Your...............

A NIGHT OF VIGIL

A terror that exceeded any of the previous alarms fell upon the Jewish inhabitants of Palestine after the "Black Thursday", when Arab soldiers seized men, women, and children on the streets of Tel-Aviv, and dragged them forcibly to the "gumruk", to deport them on the Italian vessel then in the harbor.

The deportees were not given sufficient time to get their most necessary articles. Children were wrenched away from their parents, and parents from children. Tender little creatures were sent off all alone, while their fathers and mothers were left behind in Jaffa. The "baharieh"—the Arabian boatmen who are savage and cruel enough under ordinary circumstances—interpreted the government's orders as a hint that the Jewish passengers were to be considered free game. While they conveyed the unfortunate persons from the shore to the vessel they conducted themselves in a cruel manner. They demanded money in the most threatening fashion, tore ornaments off the necks of the women, and ripped ear-rings from their ears. The transportation of the passengers took place at night, the water was rough, and the passengers were in the hands of the barbarous grandsons of the old-time pirates.

Facts expand easily in the Orient, and frightened spirits provide favorable soil for the wildest rumors. Tales were told of happenings on that night which set one's hair on end. A nine-year-old girl, according to to one report, fell overbroad during the confusion, and she was later washed up by the waves on the shores of Tel-Aviv.

On account of the events of the "Black Thursday" a large section of the populace was seized with impatience to leave the country as soon as possible, of their own free will, so as to be spared a similar experience in the future.

Immediately after this came the order from the government, declaring that all foreign subjects and citizens intending to leave the country must do so not later than December twenty-eighth. After that date the port would be closed, allowing no vessels to enter or leave.*

We could prolong our deliberation no further. We had to come to a decision. Either remain bottled up in Eretz Yisroel, penniless and barred from communication with the rest of the world, or leave on the last vessel for Egypt, there to await the end of the war. Common-sense, as well as all of our friends and neighbors, advised to follow the latter course.

There were still a few days left before our departure. I was eager to breathe in as much as possible of my new home, where it had not been vouchsafed me to celebrate the first anniversary of my coming.

All the trees in our orchard knew that I was leaving

*As it later appeared, the port was open for almost a year after this date. The final day was repeatedly postponed so as to permit another transport of foreigners to leave.

Eretz Yisroel, and every one of them contemplated me with yearning and entreaty.

"Do not forget."

I sauntered about the colony for hours at a stretch. The olive groves and the orange groves, having drunk their fill of the rains, were fresher than I had ever seen them before. The sky was as clear and pure as a sapphire gem. A velvety breeze was blowing, and the sun penetrated into every nook and cranny. The mountains of Judea once again dreamed behind their azure veils, and the pigeons circled above the school-house, the kindergarten, and the synagogue, while the "moshevah" dozed peacefully in the midday sun.

I wanted to take all this along with me: the sun, the sky, the hills, the doves, the bell near the market-place, and the singing of the children in the class-room.

When the evening of our departure came, and our things were already packed, the whole colony came to bid us farewell. There were friends and total strangers. For we were all members of one large family. They brought us dainties for the journey. One brought cookies that had been baked especially for us; another almonds. We all sat about the long, rough table that the asthmatic Mayshe had made for us, and our hearts were heavy, as we exchanged wishes and *au revoirs*. It was past midnight when the last person bid us Godspeed.

When we had been left alone, and the cold night came crawling into our room, we threw a couple of eucalyptus logs into the tiny stove, and sat there gazing at the dark faces in the flames.

We did not care to sleep. Our last night in Rehoboth must be a night of vigil. Mahmud was to arrive at about four in the morning and take us to Jaffa. We wished to drive out of Rehoboth in the dark, softly, so that nobody in the colony would see us go. We felt the grief and the shame of our departure. I felt guilty toward those who were remaining behind, and the guilt lay heavy upon my soul.

My lids began to close, when I heard the house collapse about my ears with a horrifying crash. I opened my eyes wide. It was Mahmud knocking at the door. The wagon was ready, and it was time to go.

The fire had gone out completely, and the white, silken embers lay cold and flat upon the bottom of the little oven. Deep darkness still pressed against the window-panes. It was yet more than a half-hour before the first rays of dawn.

We took our two valises, into which we had packed the most necessary things, once more took in the furniture and the walls, glanced at the Mogen David of braided corn-ears that hung all desolate, and left the house. We locked the doors, and quietly placed the key upon the window-sill of our neighbor, who was to look after our belongings in our absence. The wagon drove us through the narrow lane. The colony was immersed in gloom. Not a spark was to be seen anywhere. Only after we had left the colony did there begin to appear in the east a pale gray glow—"the wolf's tail", as the Persians call it.

"The wolf's tail" kept expanding, and behind us the "moshevah" grew white. The braying of an ass was heard, and in the yards the Arabian arbagis began to waken.

It was light when we reached the little wood that lies between Rehoboth and Vadi Khanin. Mahmud stopped the vehicle, stepped slowly down from the driver's box, and spread out his "Sejedeh" close to a bush on the road. He turned his face toward the south, in the direction of holy Mecca. He held his hands outspread, like wings, on either side of his face, and his eyes were fixed upon the earth. With ardent devotion, paying not the slightest attention to us, he murmured: "Bismi'llahi'r-rahmani'r-rahimi—in the name of Allah the compassionate, the merciful. Lord of the worlds, King of the day of judgment, Thee do we worship, and to Thee do we cry for help. Guide us on the right path."

Then he sank on his knees, and lay his head upon the earth: "Allah Akbar" (Allah is omnipotent).

When he had finished his prayers, he coolly folded his tattered "Sejedeh", clambered back to his seat, and poured forth a volley of curses upon his horse.

In the meantime the sun had thrust out a golden horn, and the horn began to grow until soon there appeared a huge disk of fire. The joyous, sun-deluged day of Eretz Yisroel had begun.

"LEHITRAOT BE-ERETZ YISROEL"

About eight o'clock in the morning our wagon entered Tel-Aviv. I sought out the building where the Anglo-Palestine Bank, though officially closed, struggled bravely to function at least in part. I found the energetic G. amidst some ten persons who were tugging at him from every direction. Since I had last seen him, his head and pointed beard had become much grayer, and his face, usually so cheerful, bore clear traces of his recent harrowing experiences. He had grown ten years older.

I told him of our decision to leave. He did not utter a word, but gazed at me in deep sorrow. In a few words he explained to me, after an embarrassing silence, the grievous difficulties that the bank was going through, and what artful means it must resort to in order to get from Egypt at least a small sum of gold so as to prevent the settlement from being utterly ruined. I asked him to give me, out of my account, enough to pay for passage to Alexandria. He counted out to me the ten Napoleons with as much care as if it were an enormous treasure.

An Italian vessel was to depart on the following day, and we decided to make reservations upon it. The prospect of having to sail by the Italian line, which was notorious for its filth and lack of comfort, was no pleasant one. But we were in no position to be particular. The worst of it was that even after having purchased a ticket and paid twice the regular price for it, one was not sure of a place on board. Since the Italian line was the only one that was still in operation between Jaffa and Alexandria, the agent, who was at the same time the Italian consul, was master of the situation. He sold tickets right and left, knowing beforehand that the steamer could not accommodate even half the number of persons. When there was no more room, he would agree to take the tickets back from the purchasers and return their money—minus ten per cent commission that he deducted for himself.

To our boundless joy a report came that the United States warship *Tennessee* was expected the day after next, and that it would transport to Egypt, in safety, all those who were forced to leave the port. The vice-consul confirmed the report, and told us, moreover, that Dr. Glazebrook, the chief consul at Jerusalem, was coming in person to see that the humane mission of the *Tennessee* be carried out without hindrance from the Turkish port officials.

On the following day, Saturday, at dawn, the exodus from Tel-Aviv began. The Italian ship arrived, and those who had purchased tickets for it hastened to reach the "gumruk" as soon as possible.

Out of the houses came persons, individually or in small groups, and set out, over sandy by-paths, with their bundles in their hands, for the port. They were ashamed to leave Eretz Yisroel publicly on a Saturday, profaning the day of rest.

Once beyond the city, the groups merged, and the road from Tel-Aviv to Jaffa was black with humanity.

All faces were grave, lips tightly pressed, all eyes filled with sorrow. They strode hastily on so as to arrive at the "gumruk" as soon as possible. Over their heads a soft, dazzlingly blue sky accompanied them, and sunbeams tagged after the multitude like mischievous urchins after a funeral procession.

We went to the American consul to learn about the *Tennessee*. At the hotel we met Dr. Glazebrook, who had just arrived from Jerusalem. The warship was expected at any moment. We stood upon the flat roof of the hotel, and gazed out upon the gold-spangled azure of the Mediterranean Sea, watching for the first signs. And when we descried a white curl of smoke, and then the tall smoke-stacks crawling above the horizon, it was like a tender greeting from home.

The tidings of the *Tennessee's* arrival circulated rapidly. Every body began to feel more at ease. The powerful arm of a great, free people was stretching across the ocean to aid and to protect.

The *Tennessee* arrived late in the afternoon, and she was to take on her passengers the following day, Sunday morning, so that we had to pass the night not in Tel-Aviv, where we usually stopped, but in Hotel Hardeg, where Dr. Glazebrook and other Americans remained in order to be ready to go to the "gumruk" early next morning.

In the evening G. came to bid us good-bye. Neither of us was able to utter a word. We clasped hands. "Lehitraot be-Eretz Yisroel." Down his sparse grayish beard trickled a large tear.

The "number" of our room was "Habakkuk". An attractive, spacious room, tidy and comfortable, with a large window and a special balcony that afforded a splendid view of orange-groves and palms, with the sea for a setting. Far into the night we sat upon the balcony and mutely spun yearnings and hopes about the stars. The large, cool stars placed a seal upon our lips. Afar, upon the waves, could be seen the *Tennessee*, garlanded with hundreds of electric lights.

The angry prophet Habakkuk did not grant me much sleep, despite the great need I had of it after the excitement and the exertions of the day. With the first gray patches of light that peered into the window-panes I was awake. My last night in Eretz Yisroel was over. Ere sunset, I shall have left the shores of Eretz Yisroel behind, with the dream of a lifetime shattered.

I went into the corridor and thence to the eastern veranda of the hotel. The city and all the surrounding vicinity were dead. Not a sign of a living creature. The east began gradually to blush, and the ruddy glow soon invaded half of the sky. Against the heavens rose a single lofty palm-tree, reaching upward, like an ardent morning-prayer.

At about ten o'clock we had already reached the port. The place seethed and roared with the din of thousands of persons. Some of these were passengers, others were friends who had come to say farewell. There were also children whose parents had been seized and deported on the "Black Thursday", while the little ones had been left to the Lord's tender mercies. And now the children were being sent to join their fathers and mothers in Egypt.

A large number of youths who knew that they would not be permitted to leave (since of subjects of enemy powers only women, children, and men unfit for military service were allowed to depart) mingled in the throng, hoping that by some chance or other they would succeed in evading the vigilance of the officials. The kaimakam, the commandant, and numerous other Turkish military and civil officials stood there subjecting every passenger to a rigid inspection. Regardless of my American citizenship, which was an envied distinction, my pockets were searched in good old Russian fashion. And contraband appeared in the guise of a letter in Yiddish. It was taken away from me, with the affable remark that I could have my choice between leaving on the *Tennessee* or waiting for the letter to go through the hands of the Turkish censor.

A motor-launch sent from the *Tennessee* was to take the passengers from the landing to the vessel. But the Jewish committee did not care to have any trouble with the "baharieh", who would have complained that the bread was being snatched from their mouths. Recalling their kindly conduct of "Black Thursday", one would hardly think that they deserved such considerate treatment.

By arrangement the "baharieh" conveyed the multitude at a price previously fixed. The moral effect the arrival of the *Tennessee* had produced upon them was evident in their behavior and their speech. They were friendly and kind to the passengers, and trembled lest anyone should enter complaint against them.

On the launch came some ten of the *Tennessee's* marines, clean-cut, natty, clean-shaved youths in blue jackets and white caps. They presented a refreshing contrast to the slovenly, dirty Arab soldiers of the "gumruk".

Within a half-hour we were clambering up the gang-plank of the *Tennessee*, and for the first time in many months were again upon American "soil".

I thought of my Napoleons. Now I no longer needed any gold, and I knew how hard pressed for gold the bank was. So I took one of the Tel-Aviv committee men aside, and gave him all that I had left—it amounted to some one hundred and fifty francs—charging him to return it to G.

The young, agile sailors helped the passengers to ascend the gang-plank. They lifted little children in their arms, supported the women and old people with the care of trained nurses, and were withal so friendly, so cheery, that the crowd fell in love with them from the first moment.

A tall, slender young man of about twenty-five, with laughing black eyes, stood at the head of the steps to prevent crowding. In Beirut he had learned a single Arabic word, "Imshi" (go), and he was specially fond of it.

"Imshi"—and he indicated to a corpulent Jewish woman that she was to turn to the right. "Imshi"—he would pat a little boy on the cheek. "Imshi"—he would gallantly bow to a high-school maiden from Tel-

Aviv. And "Imshi", in the meantime, keeps his eye upon the throng to prevent them from stepping upon each other's toes, and upon the "baharieh" who are arriving with new boat-loads of persons, lest they play some "dirty tricks". Of a sudden "Imshi" notices a "bahari", on the sly, give an elderly Jew a poke in the ribs. Whereupon "Imshi" jumps down and lands such a powerful blow upon the "bahari" that the fellow nearly topples over. "Imshi".

The transfer of the passengers lasted far into the evening, and the sky filled with stars when the screws of the *Tennessee* began to revolve, and the silhouettes of the houses in Jaffa began to recede farther and farther into the distance.

The deck of the *Tennessee* buzzed like a bee-hive, and seethed with a conglomeration of every Jewish type found in Eretz Yisroel. Patriarchs in large fur-lined hats and flowing beards, dignified merchants of middle age, women in ancient bonnets, and young women dressed in the latest fashion, wealthy persons from Russia, and professional beggars, workingmen in their blouses, students of both sexes from the Tel-Aviv high-school crowded the vessel fore and aft. In addition to these, there were many Oriental Jews whose parents for generations were born and bred in Palestine, but because they were registered as subjects of France or England, were compelled to leave the land of their birth.

The little children had a great time running merrily about among the adults and sliding upon the smooth, well-scrubbed deck.

Officers and sailors, from highest to lowest, displayed the utmost consideration and patience in making the "guests" feel as comfortable and as much at home as was possible upon board a ship that had been constructed for quite other purposes than that of a free lodging-house. They did not understand the langauge of the emigrants, but kindness and pity, on the one hand, and misery and helplessness, on the other, possess their own Esperanto. So that they managed somehow to converse, and understood each other perfectly.

It seemed as if the entire vessel—the iron railings,

the high smoke-stacks, and even the gaping mouths of the cannon—were eager to show as much friendliness as possible to these exiles.

The arrangements of sleeping-quarters for such a vast crowd was no mean task. The sailors yielded their own places. But when even this did not produce enough room for all, part of the deck was framed in and covered with canvas, thus providing a huge tent. The night was mild, and neither cold nor wind was to be feared.

The multitude was aroused early in the morning. The canvas was taken down, and the bedding quickly gathered. The orchestra took up its position and burst forth into "The Star-Spangled Banner", and a large American flag was hoisted, fluttering in the morning breeze like an earnest of free, glorious days.

The "guests" of the *Tennessee*, both young and old, stood around and listened in mute ecstasy to the national hymn of the great republic on the other side of the ocean, gazing with reverence upon the Stars and Stripes.

The day was remarkably beautiful and serene. The sea lay like a sheet of blue, transparent silk. The refugees were in high spirits. After the harassing experiences of the past few weeks in Palestine, after all their anguish and fears, they felt as if just freed from a dungeon.

The younger element strolled about the deck or else gathered in groups to sing or to "speak" with the sailors. The girls laughingly allowed themselves to be taught English words by the bluejackets, and the youthful, athletic teachers devoted themselves enthusiastically to their dark-eyed students. The older people could not find words with which to express their admiration and appreciation of the sailors' kindness. What good, spendid fellows! And such plainness. A tall, slender man passes with a gold-braided cap and numerous chevrons upon his sleeve—evidently a high officer of the ship. He pauses, bends down to a poor old woman, and asks her something in deaf-and-dumb language. The spectators fairly burst with laughter at the sight of the handsome American thrusting his fingers into his mouth, by way of inquiring whether she has had anything to eat. And he becomes to them the symbol of America, the land of which they have all heard such wonderful tales, and where their relatives dwell. And now they get a taste of free, happy America.

Directly under the huge cannon stands a Jew of about fifty, wearing a *talit*, reciting his morning prayers. He winds the thongs of his phylacteries about his hairy arms, and recites his verses with as much ease and leisureliness as if he were in his own home. After he has put on the phylacteries, he paces back and forth upon the deck and gives himself up to the raptures of prayer.

All of a sudden there is a commotion, and the crowd dashes to a corner, where a Sephardic woman has swooned. She is near accouchement, and it looks as if the *Tennessee* is going to have its passenger list increased by one.

Passage-way is made, and the doctor arrives. He examines the woman, and knits his brows. Never has the *Tennessee* been confronted with such a case. So he orders her, for the present, to be taken to the hospital cabin. Two girls from Jaffa volunteer to lead the patient thither by her arms. In the meantime the quartermaster receives a requisition for bouillon and biscuit, and we are all prepared for a "Mazzol tov" at any moment.

A few hours pass and the prospective mother reappears upon deck. It had been a needless scare. She had refreshed herself with the bouillon and biscuit, and had herself discharged from the hospital.

The "labor pains" were repeated several times during that day, and each time the quartermaster would receive a new requisition for bouillon and biscuit. Yet it always proved to be a false alarm.

The young sailors came upon a poor old blind man with a begrimed seven-year old urchin who served as his guide. So they took the pair under their special protection. It was decided, in the first place, to collect a few dollars among themselves for the "poor old Jew". No sooner said than done. And the blind old man felt a heap of silver coins in his palm.

But it was not so easy to execute their second resolution: to wash and tidy the tiny guide. The lad's fear of soap and water was overcome only when the blind man intervened on behalf of the sailors. Surely he and his son were in duty bound to pay them back somehow or other.

The little boy was taken into the bath-room and two muscular fellows washed and scrubbed him with inquisitorial instruments invented for the express purpose of torturing poor little boys from Jerusalem who are affected with "soapophobia".

When the youngster reappeared upon deck in the company of the sailors, it was difficult to recognize him. A really handsome little fellow. Before, when he was covered with the earth of Eretz Yisroel, it had been impossible to appreciate this.

The sailors were delighted with their protegé, and the tailor managed to find a remnant of blue cloth, which he at once cut into a pair of trousers for the youngster.

A young sailor, a graduate law student who intends after his discharge to set up as an attorney, gets into conversation with me. He tells me of their experiences, immediately after the outbreak of the war, when the *Tennessee* was cruising between Holland, France, and England, carrying American refugees to safety.

"You probably think that it's these people who give us the most trouble. But you're mistaken. We were much more pestered by the men and women million-aires whom we transported to England. These people here appreciate what is done for them and behave well. It's the others who proved to be real hogs. They treated us sailors as if we were butlers or waiters.

An extremely wealthy lady turned to a sailor and said peremptorily:

'Steward, carry my baggage into my cabin.' Whereupon the sailor drew himself proudly erect and replied:

'Madame, I am nobody's steward. I am a sailor upon Uncle Sam's cruiser *Tennessee.*' Others, before going to bed, would place their shoes outside the door, to have them polished, just as if they were in a hotel."

On Tuesday, the twenty-ninth of December, we reached the outer harbor of Alexandria. On all sides, German and Austrian merchant prize ships, which had been captured in the war, were rocking gloomily in the quiet waters. Since it was too late to allow the passengers to land on that day, their disembarkation was postponed till the following morning.

In order to allay the impatience of the "guests", moving-pictures were exhibited on deck that night, much to the entertainment of the crowd. There were many among the spectators who were seeing a cinema for the first time in their lives.

Preparations for landing were begun at dawn. Before the first party left the cruiser, an elderly Jew stepped upon a high box and delivered a fervent speech in Yiddish. He lauded America for the boons she was conferring upon the unfortunate and the persecuted of all the nations, and asked the whole assembly to express their gratitude unanimously. At this his hearers burst into cheering which lasted several minutes. And those cheers came from the bottom of everybody's heart.

Together with the small group of Americans that sailed on the *Tennessee*, we remained with the last ones to leave. Our launch set out for shore at just the moment when the flag was hoisted and the band struck up the national hymn.

Clear and exultant, the notes flared through the limpid air, strong and triumphant amid a collapsing world.